PRODUCT
SENSE

HOW TO SOLVE PROBLEMS LIKE A PM, ACE YOUR INTERVIEWS, AND GET YOUR NEXT JOB IN PRODUCT MANAGEMENT

PETER KNUDSON & BRAXTON BRAGG

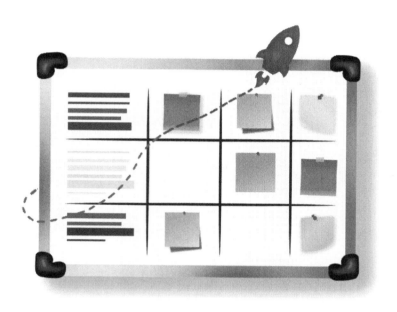

More resources and tips at

<u>ProductSenseBook.com/Resources</u>

Table of Contents

INTRODUCTION

A Bootcamp in a Book

Have you ever found yourself in a situation where you needed new computer equipment, quickly?

Perhaps you were going on an extended trip abroad and needed to ensure that you could work as efficiently as you do at home or in the office. Maybe you started to envision the difficulty of keeping up with work during your travels, knowing that your clients would expect the same level of productivity that you always provide. So you started to panic. You assessed your equipment and realized that, at minimum, you would need a new computer mouse. Sure, most people don't travel with a mouse—they use the trackpad and do just fine. Yet, your type of work requires the fine tuning that only a mouse can provide, and your current mouse is not as "travel friendly" as some of the newer models. So, you set out on a journey—an online journey to find and purchase the ideal mouse for your trip.

As usual, you begin your search by visiting Amazon.com, and sort the results by highest average customer rating. In classic Amazon fashion, it returns hundreds of similar mice from which to choose, and each result introduces a variety of different features, additional accessories, and choice of sellers (some of which seem less legitimate than others).

You painstakingly scrutinize product reviews and evaluate what other customers have learned from their purchases. "I appreciate the extra buttons," one reads. "Great traction for gaming," says another. However, you're not a gamer. As you continue to peruse the results and scan the reviews, you begin to form a mental checklist of your mouse needs and wants: lightweight, compact, rechargeable, and, ideally, Bluetooth-enabled.

You may or may not be aware of the fact that each mouse presented in your Amazon search results has enabled you to create this mental checklist. Every feature provided with these mice was the result of an extremely focused and intentional design process.

This intentional design is part of a concept called "product sense," the ability to think about products in a structured and conceptual manner. When you peruse Amazon search results you are seeing others' product sense in action, and then applying your own.

This way of thinking entails not only understanding *what* a product does but also articulating *why* it solves a particular problem and *how* it should be built in order to address that problem. It is the reason why so many mice exist—a gamer's needs may be entirely different than that of an average traveler, and an average traveler's needs may be very different from those of a traveler who needs to be able to work online very efficiently, regardless of location. Thus, from the manufacturer's standpoint, to successfully build a product it is vital to understand for whom a product is being designed, so that the user's specific needs and concerns may be successfully addressed. This is how product designers at a manufacturer exercise their product sense.

Likewise, by conducting a search for a mouse, you exercised your own inherent product sense. Your product needs triggered you to browse, filter, research, and identify your needs and concerns. Later, if you return to that product page to post a review of the item you purchased, you will have further evaluated the product based on whether or not it actually improved your life, thereby flexing your product sense muscle even further.

Product sense—and the process of empathizing with a target user's needs—extends to almost any product we interact with, including your favorite applications:

- Snapchat satisfies the unspoken need to post fun, short messages for friends to enjoy.

- Facebook encourages congregating within small, like-minded communities via its Groups feature.

- Netflix feeds the binge-watcher mentality by allowing users to skip a show's introductory credits.

Design with purpose alone is insufficient to make a product successful. Brand-new products require deep research to address real problems and innovate on the shortcomings of what is already in the market. One needs to immerse oneself in the end-to-end process of bringing new ideas to users, serve as the glue connecting the parts of that process, and be the champion that resolves problems that arise before, during, and after a new product launch.

In digital product development, product managers—or PMs—serve in this role. To become a great digital product manager who builds strong products, you must first master thinking like one.

Product managers release new products, optimize existing products, interact with customers, and attempt to understand the problem spaces in which they operate. They lead teams and garner support from the executives and the rest of the company, in order to align everyone to the same goal. PMs define the product roadmap, analyze customer behavior, and help foster positive culture within and across teams. Product managers are hired, essentially, to solve problems.

PMs aren't *necessary* in order for engineers to develop something new. However, the larger a company or the more complex the industry, the more friction there might be when deciding which direction to take or how to get something done. Building the wrong thing, or not solving an actual user need, is costly and can even sink an otherwise successful business. PMs, sitting at the center of many moving pieces—and serving as the voice of the customer—can introduce structure to an organization so that the right problems are efficiently solved.

You might be here because you can thrive on this type of puzzle solving and be comfortable working within ambiguity and organizational chaos. Perhaps you like to be at the center of an effort to create something new and meaningful. Even better if you are curious about how the sausage is made and are comfortable getting your hands dirty while making it!

Defining *"Product Sense"*

Before we go further, let's talk about the title of this book and why we chose it. We began this introductory section with an example of intentional design thinking—showing how the manufacturer's focus on intentional design (their product sense)—but we believe that a PM's product sense is much more than just design.

As you progress through preparing for interviews at most tech companies, you'll encounter "product sense" interview questions, which typically require you to break down, deconstruct, or otherwise design a part of a product. This is usually the most common type of interview question used to evaluate a PM's ability to succeed in a Product role. We agree that aptitude for "product thinking" is part of an individual's product sense, but our goal through this book is to explore the entirety of what encapsulates a PM's ability as it relates to the entire PM role. Our thesis is that a PM's product sense encompasses not only the ability to design and create new features and products, but also to optimize, execute, and lead within a product development organization.

We aim to broaden the definition of this term, and deepen your understanding of the concept of product sense, throughout this book. In Part 2, we will unpack how to prepare for your product sense interview questions, to go along with the industry definition of designing something new, but we will also cover the categories for execution, leadership, and strategy interview questions.

Our hope is that, by reading this book, you will strengthen your overall product ability—*your* product sense—and come to understand the full scope of strong product management and what life is like for product managers on a day-to-day basis. We aim to provide you with an overall understanding of product management and how that applies across different companies, industries, and products—while simultaneously helping you to adopt a PM mindset, so you can begin to see how *you* would approach the PM role you are seeking.

To step into the role of a product manager, you must possess a product sense mindset. If the previous statement has conjured up images of Luke Skywalker, struggling to follow Obi-Wan Kenobi's teachings to become a Jedi and use *the Force,* good for you! You will need to use your product sense in every area that is appropriate to the role of a PM, and this book was written to teach you to do just that.

Uncovering the Common PM Traits

In 2009, Mark Pincus—serial entrepreneur and founder of the rapidly growing social-gaming company, Zynga—tweeted a call-to-action in an effort to grow his product team:

"If [you] are a rock star in banking or consulting, apply to be the next ninja product maker."

He didn't ask for game-industry veterans to come take the reins of his products. Why did he specifically call for folks in banking and consulting?

At the time, Zynga had tens of millions of users across its various Facebook games—especially *FarmVille*, *Mafia Wars*, and *CityVille*. Users were acquired via the network effect of Facebook notifications as well as via the burgeoning engagement of the Facebook News Feed. Activity by players within Zynga's games generated massive amounts of data, allowing Zynga to adapt and evolve its games quickly based on insights and analytics.

The Zynga of 2009 wanted PMs with an inherent aptitude for data analytics, which was a very valid strategy for the time. Since then, the landscape of how products are built has shifted and evolved into varying approaches. More organizations have come to need someone to shepherd feature development and employ customer empathy, without the benefit of quick release cycles and without the wealth of data often secured by large-scale consumer apps.

Traditional sectors (for example, finance or manufacturing) have become more digitally focused and have created roles for aspiring PMs, to help flesh out their digital touchpoints and products. Needs can vary greatly from product team to product team, depending on the focus areas and complexities of the products being created. Today, there are opportunities for PMs with widely varying wheelhouses to find the right company match when applying for a PM position.

In contrast to the 2009 call for analytics-heavy PM applicants, an October 2020 PM job posting by the unicorn social-networking company Reddit described a need for individuals who could exhibit "excellent product sense" and who would excel at "driving products or toolings that involve multiple sales and marketing stakeholders."

Each individual company's hiring needs require a person with specialized traits or experience. To find that needle in the haystack and fill a crucial role, a company must first map out and post a job description. Next, job recruiters will seek out candidates who seem to be the right fit. Finally, the hiring team will interview candidates. During the interview process, the recruiters and the hiring team will assess a candidate's baseline knowledge of the fundamentals of product management, even before delving into the specific skills needed at that company.

So what does a baseline knowledge of the fundamentals of product management look like? Believe it or not, despite the many variables within a given job description, there is a common framework that we've come to gradually recognize as we built our own Product careers over the last ten years.

First, we'll give some context by sharing our own stories.

Meet Your Bootcamp Trainers

We, the authors, are product managers who first met when we joined Mark Pincus's cohort of data-driven PMs in 2012.

During our time at Zynga, the onset of social gaming drove demand for PMs to help combine UX, analytical ability, and business sense. We started our tenure as Zynga PMs on the exact same day—in the basement of their large San Francisco building, adorned with a big red banner of an American bulldog (an homage to Pincus's dog, Zinga). We spent our first two weeks in all-day "bootcamps," with approximately twenty other new PMs, learning the ins and outs of product management.

Bootcamp-style training is not a novel concept, especially at larger companies where the onboarding of new employees takes place almost every week. For engineers, this is a way to learn the ropes of a company's technology and the standard coding practices expected by the teams to which they will eventually be assigned. PMs learn about the various partners with whom they will work and the processes and decision-making frameworks that others around the company use. There's no better introduction to the work of a PM than an intensive bootcamp, taught to you firsthand by the company at which you are launching your Product career.

However, not all companies offer these elaborate, intensive training bootcamps; they are a luxury that not everyone is able to receive. If this level of onboarding is not offered by the company that hires you, you may have to learn how to manage products through the lens of your personal day-to-day responsibilities. Alternatively, you might scour the internet and read Medium posts and corporate blogs in an effort to, piece by piece, make sense of the product management landscape. Feeling your way through self-taught PM skills may leave you with knowledge gaps that will impede your ability to translate your skills between companies and across industries—and keep you from standing out in an interview.

That's why we wrote *Product Sense*. We have worked inside corporations that offered new hire bootcamps, risen to the level of bootcamp trainers, spent time at companies that didn't offer such intensive and thorough onboarding, and sat many times over in both the candidate's seat and the interviewer's seat. We've worked as PMs under many different circumstances and seen and experienced how vast and varied the call for a PM can be. Through all of this, we both relied heavily on the strong foundation we gained in that very first bootcamp at Zynga. We want to give you the edge you will need to land the PM job of your dreams; therefore, we have pooled our combined experiences to create this "bootcamp in a book" just for you.

So, who are we? Please allow us to introduce ourselves!

Peter Knudson

My foray into product management actually started as a career in game design.

I had always been a gamer as a kid, my game of choice being *Magic: The Gathering*. I met most of my friends through the game and played on a regular basis, and because of this I wanted to see if I could make a career of building games. During college I got the chance to become a game-design intern at Wizards of the Coast (maker of my favorite game, *Magic)*—learning the ins and outs of designing cards for the game that I loved. I discovered that working on game products, and learning the business behind building them, was really fascinating to me. I also liked the fact that the products and businesses do well when people are having fun.

Although I didn't stay a game designer, nor in table-top products, I did transition into digital-game product management. Throughout my career I've always stayed in game companies such as Activision, Unity, and Electronic Arts, and I've noticed that in the various facets of the gaming world, as well as in other types of tech companies, products and players are thought of in largely the same way.

I find product management to be a fascinating field because you are at the intersection of all the moving pieces of a business and how products are built, how they are sold, and how users interact with the products that they encounter. It's important for an organization to have strong PMs—PMs become very important for the success of a business. It has become one of my passions to help craft capable people into strong, logical, and crucial decision makers, which is why I took part in writing this book.

Braxton Bragg

I took a more circuitous route into product management than Pete did. Despite being a geeky kid who spent many of my weeknights and weekends playing video games, I was very fixated on a career in business and majored in Accounting and Leadership Studies during my time as an undergraduate at the University of Richmond. My goal was to work for a few years and then complete a full-time MBA program at an elite school. After a few years as a public accountant at a firm in the Washington, D.C. metropolitan area, and then as an internal auditor at the United Service Organizations (USO), I was fortunate enough to be accepted to Columbia Business School and attended from 2011 through 2013.

While at CBS, I explored multiple career paths but ultimately settled on tech because I wanted to spend my many hours at work in a place where the culture and business better aligned with my personal interests and values. The only problem was that I had no idea what to do *within* tech! I just knew that I no longer wanted to be an accountant and started trying to figure out a different path. Product management was just starting to take off at that time and, with the help of classmates and my extended network, I was able to get my first PM job at Zynga starting in August 2013.

Since those early days in Product, I've worked in several startups as well as at McKinsey & Company, working to improve the Firm's app and the publishing platform on McKinsey.com. Each job has been very different from the last, and I've learned a great deal just observing and defining how different product development teams function given varying circumstances. For the last two years, I've been coaching CBS students who are interested in product management, a role which inspired me to better define my own concept of the profession through writing and led to the initial conversation with Pete about collaborating on this book. It's been a great couple of years putting this all together!

We have done our best not only to bring perspectives from our own careers to this book but also those of other notable product leaders who have worked within many different product management contexts. Our collective experience includes B2C, B2B, developer tools, consumer products, games, and a handful of other successes and failures. We've worked as full-time employees, independent consultants, and startup advisors. We each have our share of war stories plus a few more gray hairs than we had back when we were just getting started.

Over the course of our own experiences, we noticed that there was a dire need for an in-depth, comprehensive look at product management as well as the PM hiring process. We also saw an opportunity to advance the discussion regarding the fundamental skills that PMs ought to have. Although there are some books on product management that address bits and pieces of these topics, we couldn't find any that were based on extensive experience in a variety of product development environments, written by PMs, for PMs. So we took on this challenge.

Going Forward

To start, we will equip you with the important concepts and fundamental skills that you will use to problem solve as a product manager. These concepts, which we will outline in Part 1 of this book, are essential to becoming a well-rounded PM. We will guide you through these fundamentals in a very intentional sequence that helps answer the most essential PM question, "What should we build and why?" We'll show you how to use this question to get from discovery to ideation and, ultimately, delivering a feature to users. Many of the questions that you'll be asked in interviews will involve some aspect of this process. While on the surface this information might appear to be basic, it's important to understand that it is the cornerstone of what you'll need to know (or re-familiarize yourself with) in order to appear highly competent and well-rounded during an interview.

This context is crucial, because in Part 2, we will teach you how to wield these basic concepts during recruitment for PM jobs. We have created a robust and structured, yet dynamic framework for answering product case questions. The knowledge you gain here will be applicable across all of the common case interview question categories—pertaining to product sense, product execution, and leadership. We call our method the "Compass" framework, and we derived it from our analysis of questions often asked by FAANG (Facebook, Amazon, Apple, Netflix, Google) companies as well as the rubrics upon which senior PM leaders at those companies commonly grade candidates. You will need an approach like this to demonstrate the structured thinking necessary to solve product problems.

The Compass Framework is a tool to help you think and communicate in a structured way during the interview, so that you can easily facilitate a clear conversation with your interviewer, as you answer the questions that you are posed. You'll notice that the framework maps closely to the concepts we will outline in Part 1— so not only will you have the tools you need to do well in the interview, but also the foundational knowledge to back them up.

We will also help you to understand how PMs fit into and operate within organizations. As part of the process of selling yourself to a hiring manager, you will need to construct a narrative that describes how you will bring value to a team. You will need to articulate your strengths and experience. That's why, in Part 3 of *Product Sense*, we will outline the preparation and process required to secure a new job in Product (as well as how to recognize differences between industries and companies and tailor your approach during the job hunt). Included in this section is a chapter written specifically for those who are trying to break into product management for the first time.

To further reinforce our concepts and provide some on-the-ground perspective into product management, we will share transcripts from interviews that we conducted with senior product leaders at premier technology companies—such as Google, Facebook, Twitter, Dropbox, and others—during our research for this book. These discussions will provide incredible context on what it means to be a product manager in a variety of environments, and what companies look for when they evaluate PM candidates. We've also included these interviews in bits and pieces throughout *Product Sense*, in order to give you real-world context as you make your way through the book.

Lastly, as you read, you will encounter bolded words or phrases. These are important terms used by Product teams at tech companies. It's always helpful to "speak the same language" as the folks with whom you are interviewing in order to impress upon them that you are a good fit. We have also provided them in glossary form at the end of the book, so that you can easily reference them when you need a refresher.

Preparing for a PM interview can be as laborious as preparing for the SAT or the MCAT. You might start to feel like you are mechanically reciting buzzwords or employing frameworks. In some cases, this might even be true! However, the best way to effectively interview as a PM is to intimately understand *why* PMs use frameworks, *how* they think about products, and *how* they solve problems.

The key to getting hired in product management is to first strengthen your product intuition and develop a deep grasp of the fundamentals—only then will you be ready to apply your knowledge in an interview, and take a structured approach to finding the right job for you.

PART 1

What Should We Build and *Why*?

CHAPTER 1

Everyone Has Product Sense

Think about a product that you use every day. Could you explain to someone what you like about it?

Imagine being trapped at a party and your neighbor, Bill, is talking your ear off about his new leaf blower. Now, Bill is not a PM, he's an insurance agent, but between his personal leaf-blowing preferences and his actual knowledge of every facet and function of his blower, he actually has a pretty good product sense about the leaf-blowing product that he owns.

You, along with billions of other consumers, buy and use products every day. Choosing one product from your life and discussing it shouldn't feel so daunting . . . you know what the product is and why and how you use it. Most people could easily name a product and state one or two things that they like about it, but only someone with a PM mindset (and carefully honed product sense) would be delighted to expound on the details of that product for a full forty-five-minute interview.

That is why *"What is your favorite product and why?"* is one of the most commonly asked questions in a product management interview. This question is a first line of defense used by interviewers to filter out unsuitable candidates. To answer this question effectively and thoroughly will require you to apply your product sense.

Product sense is an important skill within product management. It's the muscle you flex to ensure that you're building the right things. Without appropriate product sense, the market would be flooded with useless or redundant products. Products are built and brought to market to address user needs, and product sense is what designers and inventors use to conceptualize how to build those products.

The interview format for a product manager role is designed to evaluate your product sense in different ways. The questions can vary widely. Here are just a few examples:

- "How would you build a vending machine for the blind?"

- "What might 'Hulu for Kids' look like?"

- "Build me a service that helps coworkers play more ping pong."

- "You are in charge of a grocery-delivery app. How would you decide what new feature to build next?"

- "You are in charge of a social network and your users are leaving your platform. Now what?"

These questions can be challenging and they are only the tip of the iceberg with respect to what you will need to know in order to make a career change into product management. In Part 2 of *Product Sense,* we will go into detail about interview questions and how to navigate them. It will build on what you learn in the following chapters in Part 1.

In addition to the challenges of the interview process, another common hurdle that many of those trying to break into product management encounter is that there are few well-defined paths to follow. Unlike our engineering counterparts, who likely have specific undergraduate degrees and coding bootcamps under their belts, PMs lack (for the most part) any parallel degrees or training programs. By now, you may have noticed that most PMs don't share a cookie-cutter professional background.

Expectations of the knowledge and skills required to be a successful PM may be unclear when one is starting out. Can you make a list of the fundamentals of product management? If so, would you be able to answer interview questions in a way that clearly and succinctly communicates your knowledge of these fundamentals?

If you've done some internet research on product management, you may have stumbled upon the essays of Ken Norton, a partner at General Ventures and a former product leader at Google. He is well known for a classic essay, "How to Hire a Product Manager," one of the early essays detailing the PM traits that hiring managers should evaluate during an interview.

One skill or trait that Norton deemed tantamount for a successful PM hire is what he called "product spidey sense." These are the instincts that enable a PM to formulate good ideas about the future direction of a product. He writes, "I am a strong believer that certain people are born with innate product instincts. These people just know what makes a great product. They're not always right but their instincts usually point in the right direction."

You might believe, based on Norton's essay, that one must be *born* with product sense. "It can't be learned . . ." Mr. Norton went on to hypothesize, but he offered, ". . . it can be tuned."

We respectfully disagree that such skills can't be learned. Amazon reviewers, as we previously highlighted, utilize product sense to evaluate the products they have purchased, despite their lack of formal training. We all implicitly have this skill and (through the process of growing and practicing our product fundamentals) we *can* strengthen our intuition. To launch or advance a career in Product, you'll need to hone your own product sense, apply it in your interview, and then use it while you are on the job.

The Existential PM Problem

A common, yet simple question that aspiring PMs ask us is, "What do I absolutely need to know about product management?" This is a fair question, considering the degree to which PM roles can vary across industries and product types. To newcomers, there may be an assumption that "a PM job is a PM job," regardless of the company or industry. The fact is, this is hardly ever the case. At minimum, there are nuances and facets that must be understood in order to perform well in the role.

Despite those nuances, a PM can apply an underlying skill set when she moves from one company to another. As a PM candidate, this is great news for you, because it confirms that your focus should be on becoming a *PM generalist,* which you can tailor to fit each role and opportunity you pursue. Through our research with PMs in different industries, as well as our own experience working in various contexts, we've ferreted out the "common denominators" that every PM needs to know and distilled them down to the most basic problem that every PM encounters.

The central and most crucial problem a PM will face and be expected and required to handle with proficiency and grace is, simply: "What should we build and why?" We will refer to this question/problem as "WSB" throughout this book. How to answer this conundrum constitutes the very crux and definition of what a product manager does.

Whether you are on the job or in an interview, acting on the WSB question will require structured thinking before the work can even begin. Our aim is to teach you the kind of structured thinking and mindset you will need to adopt in order to approach answering this question as a PM— in a way that will be applicable everywhere you could go in digital product management.

A Closer Look at the WSB Question

Most product managers spend their days on a never-ending quest to determine **"What should we build and why?"**

A PM with strong fundamentals can at least make some initial progress toward answering that question, even in a company or industry that she does not know well. Product jobs generally require one to navigate ambiguity, exhibit leadership and calm temperament, and demonstrate the tenacity to deliver new features. If you can thrive within these constraints, you'll become one of the most desirable PMs on the market and will be hirable at many companies.

We believe that these skills are transferable and applicable within many different industry contexts. During our two-week bootcamp for new hires at Zynga, senior-level Product folks from various game studios repeatedly drilled us in PM best practices. "A good PM is industry agnostic," one of the presenters told us. Although we were being groomed for product management in social games, the experience and knowledge we gained has remained relevant throughout our careers. Our goal is to help you approach product management with this same intention—to become an industry-agnostic PM—because we know from our own experience that this will be the key to making you a compelling candidate at every transition point across the breadth of your career in Product.

What we are describing is a mindset and, in order to achieve this mindset, you will utilize our structured process for adeptly answering the WSB question. Can you understand a problem, influence others, and deliver the features, changes, and improvements necessary to solve that problem?

Of course you can! With the right preparation, you will not only get that next PM job but you will *excel* at it.

In an interview setting, you'll be asked questions designed to probe your ability to think about products: how you'd design or improve them, metrics you would evaluate, trade-offs you might consider, and how you'd manage execution from start to finish.

Interviewers will want you to demonstrate the end-to-end process that you would employ if you were hired. *"How would you design a travel app?"* can be boiled down to WSB. *"You observe a sudden decline in our product's daily active users. What should we do about this?"* is also a WSB problem because you must respond to a scenario with a discovery process and ultimately (and confidently) articulate a set of next steps.

Each of the next several chapters will outline our approach to solving the WSB problem and describe each concept in detail. The context and understanding that you gain will be presented within a concise framework that you can apply to various interview settings and case questions (i.e., hypothetical product questions posed by an interviewer). We'll take this application even further in Part 2.

How to Approach the WSB Problem

The following concepts will help you to build the transferable, agnostic skills you'll use to solve problems as a PM. Our goal is to help you learn to deconstruct the WSB problem down to its core components.

Understanding the core components that help solve the WSB problem is important for several reasons. First, they provide an overview of how product managers effectively and confidently approach problems, determine a direction, and decide what to build. Second, they are the basis of how to answer product interview questions. If the mechanics of what you will do *on* the job versus how you interviewed *for* the job are fundamentally different, there might be a hiring mismatch.

The basis of the WSB problem

Even though *what* is listed first in the "What should we build and why" problem, you should always start by answering the *why*. By correctly framing the problem and outlining your goals clearly, the particulars of your solution and the steps to achieving your definition of success will often follow more easily.

Our approach is top down and relies upon the fundamental skills that every technology company expects PMs to use. Think of our approach to answering WSB as a funnel beginning with the vision at the top and ending with a solution at the bottom.

Framing the WSB problem:

1. Product Vision, North Star Metric, Strategy
2. Discovering User Value and Identifying Problems
3. Prioritize
4. Execution

Product managers use these concepts, in this order, while solving problems in their daily work and over the course of developing features and new products. The purpose of this approach is to first frame the problem before diving in. By starting at a high level and then narrowing in on the specifics of your solution as you follow these steps, you will reduce the risk of an undesirable outcome.

The end goal of applying this structure is to enable you to confidently state the following for your product:

We are building [Solution] in order to solve [Pain Point] for [Persona]. This is important for the business because [Strategic theme] which relates to our [Vision], and will be measured by [North Star Metric].

We're going to revisit this statement again later on, as stating your plan concisely is critical to answering interview questions correctly.

Over the course of the next few chapters we will define each step of the WSB problem, and give you some helpful advice on how to think about and put them into practice. Since the goal of this book is to help you land a PM job, we will then transition into how to apply these concepts within our interview framework and answer PM case questions. The best responses during interviews come from those with a solid grasp of the concepts, which is why we will spend the next chapters explaining what you need to know in order to provide the optimal response. These concepts are important for utilizing the Compass Framework (our product interview case question methodology), which we will cover in Part 2.

We don't propose that our text in this part of the book encapsulates everything about product management, in every scenario. We also know that there are likely some PMs out there with different opinions on the importance of some of our concepts. That is OK. As we have stated, every PM's path and experiences are different. Our goal is to provide the right amount of understanding and knowledge for you to demonstrate great product sense—across strategy, design, execution, and leadership. In Chapter 2, you'll learn a bit about each of those areas. We believe that the more time you spend internalizing our book—as well as other PM prep materials—the more you will develop your own unique take on how to answer PM interview questions and, ultimately, how to approach the job.

Since the *why* comes first in good product management, we will begin by setting a vision, and defining your North Star.

CHAPTER 2

Product Vision, North Star, Strategy

The first thing that a product manager should do before solving any problem is to *frame* the problem. Answering the WSB problem, which is so fundamental to our work, requires particularly delicate problem framing. Before any solutions are presented—either on the job or answering an interview question related to product management—a PM should diligently define what problems are to be solved and clarify the business goals.

In the context of product management, framing a problem is articulating the constraints and assumptions that you'll use to guide your decision-making. This step is important for two reasons:

1. You can more easily facilitate productive discussions with your colleagues about where to go next.

2. You will ultimately create better solutions, products, and features because you have taken the time to evaluate the full set of paths before you and thought through the potential trade-offs, prior to taking any action.

Imagine taking another player's place in the middle of a game of chess. Before you can make your first move, you must consider where your pieces are, how many you have left, and *which* pieces are left. Only after you've assessed the state of the game will you begin your series of moves. And on top of the disadvantage of not playing the game from the start, you will have to determine what your opponent will do in reaction to each of your moves.

A product manager's role is similarly strategic. The first question one should ask is, "What problem are we trying to solve?"

As a PM, you can maximize your team's effectiveness by facilitating a rich discussion that will amplify the chances of shipping something impactful and minimize the risk of failure. If you don't examine the game board before making a move, no one else will.

Framing a problem effectively requires careful consideration of the following questions:

- What are we trying to achieve and how will it support the company's strategic goals and mission?

- What is the business outcome we are trying to achieve, or the customer use case we are trying to enable?

- What is the competitive landscape and why is now the right time to invest in specific strategic areas?

- What does success look like and how will we measure it?

- What are the specific customer behaviors we want to influence or change?

Incidentally, while interviewing for product roles, your interviewer will pay close attention to your approach as you begin to answer anything related to the "What should we build and why?" question. It will serve you well, over the course of the next few chapters, to pay keen attention to how each WSB concept is applied. The more you adopt this mindset now, the better it will shine through in your interviews.

The concepts we'll discuss in this chapter "live" within the first two steps of the WSB approach and are the key springboards to lead you into a PM mindset. They are the first steps to effectively *framing* a problem, *before* brainstorming and articulating any solutions.

Taking It from the Top: A Vision for Your Product

In 1997, Jeff Bezos wrote a letter to his Amazon shareholders. First, he recounted the impressive financial results of the previous year, which represented exponential growth over the year prior (an important metric to tech investors).

"But this is Day 1 of the Internet," he qualified. "Today, online commerce saves customers money and precious time. Tomorrow, through personalization, online commerce will accelerate the very process of discovery." Bezos wanted to paint a picture that illustrated how Amazon would evolve as the Internet matured, creating a more connected society, with emphasis on Amazon's customers and what Amazon could offer them.

"We believe that a fundamental measure of our success will be the shareholder value we create over the *long term*," he continued, setting the expectation among his shareholders of lower returns in the short term but much higher market capitalization over the long term. He summarized his pitch by saying that his company would "establish an enduring franchise" and become a household brand for years to come.

Mr. Bezos, in this letter, was communicating his vision for his company and providing a glimpse into Amazon's future. While he penned this letter as a CEO, creating and communicating a vision is something that anyone who aspires to build something new must be able to do, regardless of his or her role.

Thus, a product manager must be capable of drafting a vision for a product, a feature, or anything else that needs to be built. Your stakeholders are your company's leadership, other PMs, and the team that will help you develop your product. All of these stakeholders need to understand what will be built and be on board with it. A vision helps frame problem statements at the highest level; if everyone can clearly see the goals, subsequent steps such as designing the feature or product become more productive and likely to succeed. When stakeholders *aren't* aligned to the vision, you must facilitate discussions to resolve the misalignment early in the process—this will minimize undesired changes in direction later (often called **"churn"** or "thrash"), which can be costly both in terms of dollars and your credibility.

Let's look at some more examples of tech companies and their visions:

Company	Vision
Unity	We believe the world is a better place with more creators in it.
Facebook	Give people the power to build community and bring the world closer together.
Slack	Make work life simpler, more pleasant and more productive.
Snapchat	We contribute to human progress by empowering people to express themselves, live in the moment, learn about the world, and have fun together.

These are all actual vision statements. Each company's vision statement is supposed to be the overarching frame that guides the work that its employees do: how they acquire new users and customers, what their products look like and how users interact with them, how and what the product development teams build with their resources, and so on.

As a PM on a product development team, when considering new features, you will need to think about and clearly communicate (in a short and sweet pitch) how you envision the end state of your feature. Let's consider an example: a simple signup flow by which new users begin to use a website.

We want our signup flow to be frictionless and enjoyable.

Having an easy and delightful experience when a user first interacts with your ecosystem sounds great, doesn't it? It also probably leads to more users completing signup, exploring your site, making a purchase (hopefully), and developing a habit of longer-term engagement. Such actions can help you concretely evaluate progress toward your vision, which is the next step in our process.

The North Star Metric: Measuring Progress Toward a Vision

Product managers (and others tasked with determining the direction of a project) often fail to clearly determine what success will look like if it is achieved. The vision statements we previously examined for companies such as Amazon and Facebook were, to say the least, quite lofty. Inspirational, perhaps, at a 10,000-foot level—

yet, not necessarily actionable by most teams in the course of their day-to-day work. Measuring success is the quantitative part of establishing a vision.

What metrics would you expect to see moving up and to the right as you make progress toward your vision? If the vision is growth related, you might want to monitor **active users** on a daily, weekly, or monthly basis. Perhaps you have further defined an active user as someone who adds items to their digital shopping cart or posts a comment on your social platform. If you are trying to create an engaged community, sessions per week or time in the app (sometimes called "session time") are often good measures. North Star Metrics need to be correlated to the desired business outcome and long term goal, and agreed upon by everyone on the team, because without everyone working toward the same goal or playing the same game, the momentum can't be realized.

The single best measurement tool for determining whether your product is performing as it should is the **North Star Metric**. The North Star Metric is a "guiding light" within your product that helps you to know if you are achieving your goal. Just as the North Star in the night sky helps people navigate when they are lost, this metric clarifies whether or not your releases are making an impact. Setting a vision for your product as well as a metric by which you will measure success are two very important pieces of the WSB approach—and they should always be considered in tandem.

For example, Uber's North Star Metric is the total number of completed rides per day. Company leadership determined that, given its operating model, Uber will be successful if it can continue to show growth in this metric. We can assume that a completed ride means that a customer paid Uber for the ride, the driver was compensated, and Uber (since it takes a percentage of the price of the ride) earned its incremental revenue. The additional hope is that both the rider and driver were happy at the end of their transaction, and the rider will use Uber again.

Let's look at some of the other companies we listed above and try to identify their North Star Metrics:

Company	Vision	Metric
Unity	We believe the world is better with more creators in it.	# of active creators per month
Facebook	Give people the power to build community and bring the world closer together.	average # of engagements with content, per user, per day
Slack	Make work life simpler, more pleasant and more productive.	monthly retention of organizations on the platform
Snapchat	We contribute to human progress by empowering people to express themselves, live in the moment, learn about the world, and have fun together.	# of Snaps created per day

A good North Star Metric takes into account longer time horizons. It shouldn't be defined by something granular, such as the use of specific features, that its importance declines within a year or less. A North Star Metric is something that should be more or less timeless, on the scale of several years or more. Ideally, a North Star Metric won't change, and it will encapsulate an aggregate of all the operations of a business into one, measurable KPI.

That said, a North Star Metric might change if a company's vision or strategy shifts or if market conditions fluctuate. While a North Star Metric is your guiding light, sometimes you need to identify a new star and change direction. But this should only happen in the case of a very significant change in circumstances.

Of course, these metrics apply at the company level or to very large business units within each company. Product teams can establish metrics, and goals for those metrics, more granularly for projects or initiatives directly relevant to their work. Defining success at the feature level is an essential skill (even for very junior PMs). If we look at the example given earlier in this chapter, related to creating an enjoyable signup flow, we could define success like this:

By improving our signup flow, more users will complete account creation, leading to a higher number of active users.

We've now discussed how a PM outlines a vision and measures success against it. We've reviewed examples of each of these concepts at a high level (company) and at a lower level (feature). It's important to note that, when framing problems at the feature level, the metric or goal should also tie back to the overall business goal. For instance, in the signup flow example, the feature increases the number of signups, which could support an overall company goal of having more engaged users because there is a larger overall number of users available to engage.

A clear vision is critical, and having a clear method for measuring progress toward that vision is fundamental—both are essential for good problem framing. Once these are established, PMs and other leaders can exercise their strategic minds to figure out how to actually get there.

Example: Mobile Game KPIs (Braxton)

While working on the mobile game Yahtzee with Buddies at Scopely, we decided that our North Star Metric should be the total number of turns played. If you're not familiar with the game, the structure (except the gameplay itself) is similar to Scrabble: 1-on-1 competitive, asynchronous, remote play leveraging an ad-monetization model. Ads are shown in between turns. You cannot play your turn until after I play mine, and vice versa. Assuming nothing is wrong or out of balance in the game, an increase in turns should result in increased revenue for the company (from additional ads shown) and stronger engagement and retention, since each turn played will notify the opposing player that he can take a turn and those notifications drive players to return to the app. This helped us focus our roadmap and also helped us better understand our customer engagement, because we looked at everything through this lens.

Connecting Vision to Strategy

To make consistent progress toward a high-level vision, you need a slightly more concrete and actionable plan. As obvious as that may sound, crafting a coherent strategy is not easy. Product development—the features that you build and the new products that you ship—will ideally stem from the strategy that your team follows.

One great aspect of product management is that PMs usually have a seat at the table when strategy is discussed. Executives, and other important business leaders, tend to listen when we explain what must be built in order to address market gaps or to make progress toward the mission.

Let's consider an example of strategy related to a company's vision.

In 2013, a little company called Tiny Speck was preparing its "preview version" of a new communication tool called Slack. The company's CEO, Stewart Butterfield, authored a blog post to both inspire his team and announce publicly his vision for what Slack would try to achieve in a world already full of communication tools. The blog post was titled "We Don't Sell Saddles Here." The title alludes to his comparison of Slack to a hypothetical saddle company. Such a company might position itself to sell a better saddle for horse riders by constructing its saddles using top-grain leather or prioritizing rider comfort. However, what the company should be selling is horseback riding; in other words, the entire experience and the thrill of it. So, for Slack, Butterfield's vision was not to sell a better communication tool but to create a better and more productive working experience.

To achieve this vision, he outlined several key elements of Slack's strategy. Take a look at this excerpt from the post:

- *We want them to become relaxed, productive workers who have the confidence that comes from knowing that any bit of information which might be valuable to them is only a search away.*

- *We want them to become masters of their own information and not slaves, overwhelmed by the neverending flow.*

- *We want them to feel less frustrated by a lack of visibility into what is going on with their team.*

- *We want them to become people who communicate purposively [sic], knowing that each question they ask is actually building value for the whole team.*

—Stewart Butterfield, CEO, Slack,
"We Don't Sell Saddles Here"

The core tenets of the strategy—ease of use, informational transparency, and effective communication—determined how the product team would prioritize feature development. As we have said, vision leads to strategy and strategy helps define the product. Progress toward the goals serves as feedback to validate the strategy and dictate any changes.

Product managers need to be strategic thinkers, especially as they gain more seniority. Although it can be difficult to switch contexts—from thinking about the minute details of a feature to planning a strategy with broader scope—demonstrating that you have an aptitude for thinking in this way will help you stand out in interviews as well as grow your career inside your product team.

Strategic thinking is about identifying an advantage that, if exploited, will lead to success. When crafting a strategy, a PM should always consider:

- What are competitors doing and how have they solved similar problems?

- Do we have any proprietary advantages (technology, data, etc.) that we can use to innovate?

- Where are the industry headwinds and how can we avoid them?

- Are there new technologies on the horizon that we can start planning for now?

In product management, we sometimes use the word "themes" to refer to the different strategies the team comes up with. When planning product roadmaps, establishing themes rather than individual features may help establish a clearer link between the vision and product development. Once you have attained internal alignment at the theme level and have clarified the goals with stakeholders, the features that you plan to build and execute will ultimately be focused in the right direction—so long as they fit within those themes. The list above illustrates how to think about themes within which a PM could execute in order to achieve their **KPIs** (key performance indicators: the metrics that help measure the business or product health).

Strategy not only applies at the highest level, you can and should think about strategies even at the individual feature level. Let's revisit the signup flow from the vision section with an example of a more granular strategy:

Investing in more supported login types, highlighting our commitment to privacy, and decreasing the number of steps in our signup would increase conversion of visitors to new accounts and ultimately lead to a higher number of active users.

Tying It Together

As we have covered in this chapter, problem framing is the first and essentially the most important step in effective product management. It is absolutely critical that you dedicate the time to gather all of the important context, prior to making decisions. When considering how to most confidently tell your team, "this is what we should build, and why," articulating a strong vision and strategy is a key first step. The same is true for any question that you might be asked during the interview process; your interviewers want to know how you frame problems before you propose solutions or new designs.

To be a leader in product management is to be a strategic thinker and visionary, and demonstrating planning at a high level is what will make you a standout candidate. Strategic thinking and goal setting are valued highly when hiring managers test for structure in your proposed development process. We have outlined for you a great first step as you begin to frame the WSB problem, as noted in Chapter 1 *(Vision, North Star Metric, Strategy)*. Next, we will look at the second step in the framing process, by uncovering opportunities to deliver user value.

CHAPTER 3

Discovering User Value and Identifying Problems

In the last chapter, we discussed problem framing and using vision, strategy, and success criteria to determine themes to invest in. In this chapter, we'll consider how to generate specific opportunities to achieve these goals. In other words, we'll unpack the *what* that comes after the *why* (not in the question, but in actual practice) in the WSB problem.

Determining what to build can depend on many factors but should begin with who uses your product and the problems with which they are struggling. Users have needs and use products to address them. Eric Ries, the author of *The Lean Startup*, said it well: "We must learn what customers really want, not what they say they want or what we think they should want." In other words, a good PM not only listens to customers and builds features based on those conversations, but also employs empathy in order to uncover the implicit problem behind their users' words. This is what leads to successful product development. Discovery is the process of ensuring that the right questions are asked so that the users' problems can be solved.

A PM with deep empathy for her users is ready to initiate a discovery process to figure out the *what*. Strong features are built when sufficient time is allocated to discovery and design.

Empathy for Your Users

Empathy is absolutely central to product management. Empathy, in our context, is an intimate understanding of users and why they need to use a particular feature or product. Users have needs due to some inefficiency in their **workflow** (the usual order of operations for achieving a task), and that inefficiency must be addressed.

As product managers, we're not always the end users of the products we manage. A PM working on Gmail or Microsoft PowerPoint likely *does* have the advantage of intimate experience with the product even before she begins working on it (although she must be careful not to equate the experiences of every user to her own, a pitfall for many PMs working on consumer products). It is much simpler to determine pain points or potential opportunities if you fall into your product's target market.

For many PMs, such as those working on B2B products, or any product built for a different type of user than themselves, insights can be less natural to come by. This is why empathy is important. An empathic PM understands the problems that a user is experiencing, without directly being in the user's position. When discovery happens first (as it should, coupled with empathy), some of the most important problems that a user might encounter may be avoided entirely. Thinking with empathy will help you to avoid many pitfalls in the products you develop.

Let's examine the different ways that PMs use and exercise empathy and how they help to determine the "what and why" when brainstorming and designing features.

The PM's role in the design process

On most product development team rosters, you'll find at least one designer. Often, that person focuses on designing and building the right feature or the right version of a feature. She thinks about things like usability, accessibility, and consistency across other features and potentially other products within the company. Design and Product often are individually at their best when they have defined an efficient and complementary partnership. So what does each bring to the table?

A PM should provide justification that a prioritized problem needs to be solved, including (but not limited to): business cases, vision statements, and a discovered user problem or direct ask from a customer. A designer (along with the engineers) is a fellow problem solver who works to satisfy the issue in a user-friendly and technically efficient way. As the connective tissue within the development team, the PM needs some awareness and understanding of design as well as user empathy in order to effectively facilitate and lead the problem-solving process.

So, how does the PM employ that empathy for her users in her daily activities? Let's first look at how a PM develops and maintains empathy.

Exercising empathy through analysis of other products

When examining other products (competitor's products, new entrants, adjacent products, etc.) a PM will use empathy to determine the good, the bad, and the ugly of each through the lens of a user other than herself.

An experienced product manager can easily distinguish between a good product and a lousy one and articulate that distinction. User empathy, in this context, means understanding the needs and desires of a hypothetical user of a given product and also with the development team that built that product. A good PM must develop a sixth sense for understanding successful features or products as well as unsuccessful ones. Why? Because product rollouts that miss the mark can result in negative impacts to retention and engagement, but a PM with strong product sense can evaluate the root cause of any issue and learn from it.

You have probably browsed online reviews for products or restaurants. Perhaps you have written your own online review. If you have ever lamented that something you bought had one big, glaring design flaw, you have practiced user empathy. If you have gone a step further and discussed or written about how you would correct that design flaw, then you have flexed your muscle as a product visionary.

Have you ever stopped to think about the products you use? Why do you favor one backpack over another? What caused you to delete that app you downloaded? This type of reflection is at the core of the product manager's mindset.

Breaking down empathy

As PMs ourselves, we have found it best to break empathy into two component parts: **user understanding** and **behavior prediction**.

User understanding is the ability to comprehend a customer's pain, problems, and goals. PMs employ user understanding as part of their product sense and develop hypotheses about what makes achieving the customer's goals difficult (or slow) to reach.

In practice, using product sense on an existing product means performing an analysis of a product's strengths and weaknesses, breaking down the design choices, and mapping them to a hypothetical user's needs.

Behavior prediction is the process of trying to anticipate how a user might react to a change in a product or system. When a product manager understands behavior patterns very intimately—perhaps through prior experiments or other available data—she can more accurately estimate how a new feature (or some other optimization) might impact product experience and the key metrics.

Product managers are constantly thinking about their users and how to evolve their products to better serve their users' needs. Let's consider this example:

> Google Flights, a website and service that compares similar flights across different airlines, has built several features with the price-sensitive user in mind. This type of user wants the best deal and a common reason for ending a session without making a purchase is the anxiety associated with overpaying. Google has attempted to solve this user pain point with price alerts, graphs of historical prices, and predicted future prices, as well as the ability to search nearby airports for a better price.

In the above example, Google PMs exercised user understanding by realizing that existing solutions didn't sufficiently cater to price-sensitive folks, which created an opportunity for their product. Dissecting product sense entails understanding the goals of the user, anticipating the problems they will encounter when attempting to achieve their goals, hypothesizing a problem fix, and measuring a behavior change as a result of a successful improvement.

- **User goal**: The user wants to buy a flight that satisfies their travel plans at a fair price.

- **Problems**: The user might want to know how the current price compares to previous or future prices but would have to check on multiple occasions to establish this trend in his mind. He might go to other websites to check various rates, which can be laborious and time consuming (and ultimately lead to purchasing elsewhere).

- **Hypothesis**: Giving users more data would improve their confidence in ticket prices. Through surveys, reviews, and contacting the company, users have asserted that ticket alerts for price drops would fix their problem and bring them closer to achieving their goal of price assurance.

- **Success metric:** If their hypothesis was successful, Google Flights would see higher conversions on tickets and fewer sessions before a booking is made.

Structured analysis of existing products is an essential practice for PMs. The above example is one potential framework for deconstructing existing products in order to build user empathy.

Strengthening User Empathy

No one should expect a product manager to deeply understand the needs and problems of every customer on day one.

A good product manager knows that she likely has gaps in her understanding or even biases that she must overcome in order to view her products objectively. Paul Graham is one of the most widely read product-thought leaders and a founder of Y Combinator. In his essay, "Six Principles for Making New Things," he advises early-stage startups to "launch as soon as you can, so you start learning from users what you should have been making."

We agree with his sentiment. Product development is a cycle of hypothesizing how the user will react, shipping an experiment, and then learning more about the user's behaviors and evolving needs. The more that this cycle is repeated, the higher the potential for improvement during each iteration. PMs are uniquely positioned to continually learn about their users and offer features that will provide value to their users.

Breaking down products to their component parts

At Zynga, we not only analyzed games that Zynga had previously launched but also games created by competitors for the purpose of learning from or "fast following" them. This practice makes sense in many different contexts and is also an excellent way for aspiring PMs to build their product sense.

Physical strength and endurance can be increased through training. The same concept can be applied to product sense. One practical way to do this is to perform a **product audit** on software or other products that you use or otherwise see in the wild.

A product audit consists of evaluating the UX of your target product through the eyes of a new user and trying to glean insights about why the product was built in that particular way. To perform a product audit, simply download an app or go to a website (creating a new account, if necessary), all the while paying very close attention to what you learn about the product's purpose and how to use it.

For services that are sufficiently large in terms of feature set—such as Facebook, Google Maps, or Spotify—you might perform the audit on specific features and how they are introduced or used within a subsection of the platform, since these individual parts would have a separate **roadmap** and success metrics.

Even if you are not building a social network or map program, you might still be interested in how these companies enable users to safely and easily create new accounts, or manage push notifications or email communications. Your approach could vary substantially based on the nature of your product or what you're working on at a given time.

While performing a product audit, it's essential to take note of these categories:

- **User expectations:** What is the expected value that the service would bring to the user? What is the value proposition, and why would someone use it?

- **User persona and problem:** Understanding what types of users the value proposition speaks to and the problems these users have.

- **New user flow:** Gauging how much friction the onboarding flow exhibits, and taking note of the friction points. If the onboarding flow is painful, you risk losing users before they've had a chance to engage.

- **Core value loop:** What steps might a user take on a regular basis to get some value back from the product?

- **Magic moment:** For users, at what point do things "click" to make them feel that the product is providing value?

- **Retention mechanics:** Did the developers purposely create flows that incentivize subsequent usage of the product?

- **Growth mechanics:** Were users incentivized, either intrinsically or extrinsically, to invite others to use the product or service? Intrinsically meaning their enjoyment of the service would improve. Extrinsically meaning they would get some form of commission or reward for successful referrals (or "invites").

Product managers contextualize their findings during product audits with comparable **benchmarks** (i.e., similar concepts in other products) in mind. If multiple products within the same industry all have Feature X, then we describe Feature X as **table stakes**— meaning that it is more or less required in this particular space in order for the product to be successful, or a market leader, due to existing expectations within that market.

A related concept is **best practice,** which is the optimization built on top of a table-stakes feature. For example, a hotel-booking site typically allows the user to search for prospective dates and returns a list of available rooms on those dates. The search results are table stakes but a best practice might be to show a set of recommended listings on top, personalized according to the user's preferences.

Finally, during an audit, if you observe a feature that delivers value for the user and isn't generally found in other related services, it might be a **differentiator.**

At Zynga, we were in the habit of continually doing audits (we called them deconstructions) of new games that hit the market—our own, as well as those released by our competitors. In the game industry, executives want to be sure that they understand the sets of features that make any games successful so that they can apply that understanding to their own games (both live and not yet released). This is for two reasons: first, to learn these best practices before entering a new game genre; and second, to identify the minimum set of features they would need to plan for (and support or allocate resources for), and how long it could take to ship the first version.

During the development of *FarmVille 2* (the sequel to *FarmVille,* Zynga's most successful game), another developer, Supercell, released a game called *Hay Day* on mobile devices that successfully replicated many of the gameplay mechanics of *FarmVille. Hay Day* became a massive hit. A Zynga PM was tasked with deconstructing it, in order to identify the Core Value Loop (a key factor of a product audit, as defined in the product audit categories, above), and to determine how different it was from *FarmVille 2.*

Conducting product audits is a great way to think about products holistically and to strengthen your own user empathy skills. User empathy is one of the most fundamental aspects of product sense. If you can apply this aspect of product sense in one industry, like games, you can also use those skills to prioritize in other industries such as ad tech, developer tools, e-commerce, or any other type of product or service that involves an end user with a goal. Good product design is not only about creating an intuitive user interface, but it is also about creating workflows that help the customer achieve their desired goal—by reducing or eliminating any problems they might encounter along the way.

Segmenting Different Types of Users

We've established that user empathy is an incredibly powerful skill, one that is essential for all successful PMs to possess, but the story doesn't end there. Often, products have more than one type of user. PMs must become adept at recognizing their products' users and segmenting them into distinct groups that share similar characteristics. Doing so can help a PM to personalize experiences or focus design efforts to serve a particular group or multiple groups. In the PM discipline, there are a variety of ways to approach this. Choosing the right method by which to frame one's users is considered a "discovery" step because it informs the work that must be done before one starts building product.

There is no single universal way that PMs select the customers they will target. Depending on the situation, the methods that might be used to segment customers into groups can and will change. We're going to look at four types of customer groups:

1. Users
2. Customers
3. Personas
4. Cohorts

A PM might choose to think about her product's end users in these segmentations. When designing an advanced feature, you might want to segment the potential users of that feature into **cohorts** based on their **engagement** level (how often they use the service or product). In another instance, you might use a **persona** to saliently describe the user whose **pain points** you are trying to fix. Each of these user terms has its own usage and context. Let's take a look at each one.

Type One: Users

We've spent some time discussing users and their needs. For your product to be relevant, you will have users. Users are individual people who interact with your product in order to solve a problem or address a need.

Entrepreneurs often cite a classic rationale for why they have created a certain product or service: "I was trying to do X and encountered problem Y, so I created my product in order to make it easier for myself and other people in my situation." This makes for a great story when raising venture capital. The entrepreneurs have an easy task when it comes to understanding at least some of their users, because they've been in the same shoes.

As a PM working for an existing company, however, your role may not be so simple. When Braxton was a new product manager at Zynga and working on *Hit It Rich!* (a social slots game with a user base of people from various backgrounds and of various ages), the key user group was comprised of American-midwestern women aged forty-five to sixty-five. As a thirty-year-old man with an MBA, living in San Francisco, Braxton's understanding of those users did not come easily, at first. Consider how challenging a role might be for a PM who:

- Has never had a pet but is working for an organic dog food company

- Doesn't like sports but works on a sports betting app

- Is not a parent but works on a product that focuses on childcare

It is not uncommon for product managers to find themselves in situations where their product's users may feel very foreign; nevertheless, it is the PM's responsibility to learn more about these groups and develop the ability to empathize with them, in order to better understand and meet their needs.

Type Two: Customers

What is the difference between users and customers? Quite simply, not every user is a customer. Many products and services in today's digital world are free to use, at least initially. For example, most Gmail users do not pay to have or use their accounts; however, Google monetizes them by placing relevant ads in their inboxes, or by charging for additional cloud storage if the usage limit is exceeded. A typical **freemium** model might only monetize a small percentage of its users, perhaps less than five percent, but it may rely upon its nonpaying users for other purposes, such as:

- Community scale/network effect

- Ad monetization: Although not directly providing revenue, free users can still be a source of revenue when served ads from other companies. *Words With Friends* earns most of its revenue from ads.

- Word-of-mouth acquisition: A particularly vocal and influential user can drive new acquisition just by singing the praises of your product on social media or to a valuable in-person network.

- Effects on paying users: In a gaming setting, free users are still valuable for the interactions they have with paying users. In *Clash of Clans*, for example, free players make great punching bags for paying players who are willing to spend thousands or millions of dollars to be the best and dominate their opponents.

Of course, non-paying *users* can become paying *customers*. For example, Weebly is a website editing and hosting platform that is considered free-to-use but functions very differently from most free mobile or web games. Weebly acquires new users by offering a very powerful free website, then gradually upsells users to paid subscriptions based on their individual needs. For example, a small business owner might set up a site on Weebly's free platform in order to sell a single item but, as his business becomes more complex, he might upgrade to a paid plan that supports his growing catalog of products and offers lower transaction fees.

Alternatively, for a membership organization, the free site might support a small number of members (<100); but, as the organization grows in popularity, a more robust plan might be required to support a username/login model and many hundreds or thousands of members.

In short: users are the people who are engaged with a product, and customers are the subset of those users who give you money.

Type Three: Personas

Differentiating between users and customers becomes easier when you consider a tool that is commonly employed by digital marketers: personas.

Personas can help simplify how you view your universe of users by making them a bit more tangible and relatable—in other words, by humanizing them. It can be very easy for a product manager to start to view her users and customers as mere statistics, after all, that is how they are typically represented in the data and in a PM's day-to-day work experience. However, a PM can take a step back and remember for whom she is developing products by creating fictional archetypes that bring the data off the page and bring her customers to life.

Remember the forty-five to sixty-five-year-old-midwestern women we referred to previously (Braxton's key demographic when he worked on the Zynga slots game)? This group could be represented in the following way:

- *Name:* Delilah Pritchett
- *Occupation:* Small business owner

- *Age:* 52
- *Sex:* Female
- *Location:* Duluth, Minnesota
- *Characteristics:*
  - Wants a distraction from the demands of running her business; ideally, something that helps her remember simpler times and some of the brands she enjoyed during her childhood.
  - Doesn't want to have to figure out complex game mechanics.
  - Enjoys meeting other people of similar backgrounds and with similar interests.
  - Generally conservative in her spending but OK paying for a better experience in her games from time to time.

Personas, or profiles, like the one above can help a product manager and other members of a product development team better understand and identify with key user groups. Armed with this knowledge, they can then roadmap particular features that will suit a persona's identified characteristics or needs.

Type Four: Cohorts

Another way that Product Managers, or other members of product development teams, might group users is by cohorts. This word can have many meanings but we should distinguish it from personas by noting that cohorts are typically less personal but are more useful for analysis and segmentation. Although two personas might, at first glance, appear very different, they could very well be in the same cohort based on some shared characteristic or metric.

Types of cohorts you might encounter and discuss as a PM may include:

- All of the users who started using the product on a particular day

- Users who have spent more than a certain dollar amount in the product

- Users who have retained (continued using the product) for a certain period of time

Really, a cohort can be any group with one or more shared characteristics that helps you understand how your product is being received. It is a way to determine what's working now, and what you might improve.

Peter's example: cohorts vs. personas

The type of segmentation done on users depends considerably on the industry in which the product operates, as well as the culture of the Product team. I have two distinct examples from my career that illustrate stark differences:

Unity, a B2B development tool for game developers, began implementing persona thinking into product discovery during my time there. They did so because they knew that, inside a game studio, the roles and responsibilities of each member of the development team can be very different; yet, any one of them could be a user of the software. So, analyzing each feature with the mindsets of different personas helped shape the UX thinking that went into each feature. In other words, by defining personas, Unity "got to know" typical game developer team members very well, which helped them to understand how and why any given member might use their software.

Conversely, at Zynga, the product development approach was very analytical and, typically, PMs examined behavior based on cohorts, grouping each user by a unique characteristic such as the date or week the user started playing or how much money he or she had spent on in-app purchases (low, medium, or high). Within those cohorts, they would examine player behavior and make updates or optimizations based on their findings.

Pain Points: Jerry Goes to Safeway

Jerry, a man who likes to meal prep, is taking his usual Sunday walk to Safeway, shopping list in hand, to pick up the new week's groceries. Feeling adventurous this week, Jerry has gotten creative with his menu, which will require a selection of items that aren't already available in his pantry. He also needs other sundries. As he makes his way to the store, he worries that he will forget something important or be unable to carry everything home. He can't spend too much time browsing the aisles, as he will need to finish his meal prepping in time to get a good night's sleep. Tomorrow he has a 6:00am call with colleagues in Helsinki.

We're all familiar with Jerry's concerns here. Finding what we need in a store never seems to happen as quickly as we desire.

Furthermore, we sometimes leave without finding everything that we originally set out to buy.

In the following sections, we're going to apply this example scenario as a basis for diving deep into understanding product problems and the pain points that represent them. By the end of the chapter, you should be able to articulate in a structured way how you would improve the grocery store experience for Jerry.

Earlier in this chapter, we demonstrated the importance of identifying specific user groups, and the various ways they can be segmented. Not only is this skill an instrumental step in the product development process, it is a key piece of knowledge for you to demonstrate during your PM interviews. If you don't understand the person you are designing a product for, you will be heading down a rough path.

Following our WSB method, the next logical step is to address the problems faced by the user group. You'll utilize your product empathy and UX skills to deep-dive early on in the design process— to head off potential user problems before they ever materialize.

Impact is the PM's responsibility

PMs want to pinpoint and tackle the most impactful problems.

Impact means bringing value to the customer by allowing her to do something more efficiently than before. To add value, one needs an intimate understanding of why processes are inefficient. You can identify impactful improvements by emphasizing the users' journey, which is just one important step in the discovery process PMs take.

You will use this information during your interview process, when faced with design-related questions.

Let's define and discuss these inefficiencies (also known as "pain points," which we'll look at in more detail shortly) and how to identify and prioritize alleviating the most acute user pain by outlining some frameworks that help quantify the impact. The best way to illustrate pain points is through our "grocery store problem" example, which we began to introduce earlier with our new friend, Jerry.

Let's talk about pain points

Product managers find themselves discussing pain points nearly every day. As ubiquitous as the term is among product development teams, it is often misused or ill-defined. Here's our preferred definition for this term.

> *A pain point is an obstacle on the journey a user takes between*
> *his starting state and his goal state.*

Teams want to identify pain points because, if they can address them, they will create value for their customers. However, to fully understand where pain points exist (and where they don't), the problem needs to be accompanied by the **starting state**, the **end state,** and a **goal.**

Jerry will experience many different pain points during his shopping trip. How can you, as the product manager, know when he has experienced a true pain point and when he has merely encountered a necessary step in the process of acquiring the items on his unique shopping list?

It's feasible that a pain point *doesn't* exist at a particular stage in the process. A user expending some effort to complete an action doesn't necessarily mean that he has encountered a pain point.

As a product manager, it is your job to identify where pain points exist and whether they detract from the user's value. If they detract, then the **friction** should be evaluated, and the work to resolve the pain points should be prioritized and solved.

Let's dissect the definition of a pain point within the context of product management and look at the following critical terms in reverse order (you'll soon understand why).

> *A pain point is an **obstacle** on the journey a user takes between his **starting state** and his **goal state**.*

Goal state

Focusing on the goal state first enables you to consider the reason that the user is on this journey in the first place.

A goal state describes the user's desired outcome, while also articulating how that user measures the degree of success achieved. **Success criteria** are paramount for understanding what your users' goals are. It's important to note that the goal state can occur even after a product's role in the process is complete. For example, while buying a pair of sunglasses on an e-commerce site may represent a conversion, the user's goal state is that—while wearing them—the sunglasses block the sun effectively and the purchaser can enjoy his time at the beach. So, what is Jerry's goal state?

Goal state (incomplete): Jerry goes grocery shopping.

Achieving an incomplete goal state, such as the one above, may be simple but could be misleading or not include sufficient detail. Jerry could walk in, buy a Coke, and call it a day. He went grocery shopping; thus, the incomplete goal state was achieved. On the other hand:

Goal state (complete): Jerry goes grocery shopping and buys all of the items on his list in under thirty minutes.

The complete goal state is more robust and has measurable outcomes. Jerry completes his trip and is happy that he could return to his house in time to meal prep for his busy week. As a product manager, you could even track his total time shopping and his list-completion rate, as part of your KPIs for your grocery store. The term "KPIs" is shorthand for "key performance indicators" and these are often used at tech companies during goal-setting exercises in order to measure progress against objectives. Whether you like it or not, you'll likely become very familiar with this term if you become a product manager at a tech company.

Starting state

Our second term from the definition of pain points above, a starting state is the point at which the user's journey begins: the customer has identified their goal and is about to take their first step on the path to achieving it. Starting state is all about the moment that a potential customer has the *intention* to act. So, what is Jerry's starting state?

Starting state (incomplete): Jerry grabs his shopping cart at Safeway.

Actually, Jerry's true starting state is well before he arrives at Safeway. If you conceptualize the starting state at a point too late in the user's process, you might miss some critical information that would help solve a key problem. Jerry always does his shopping on Sundays, so his starting state begins with his *intention* to shop. Note that this is quite a few steps back from his first interaction with Safeway. A more accurate approach would be:

> **Starting state (complete):** It's Sunday and Jerry begins planning his meals for the week.

Let's look at a real-world example of thinking further ahead to find a complete starting state. In an urban environment, fewer potential customers have cars and, for those that do, finding parking can be an intensely frustrating and time-consuming experience. Mollie Stone's, a grocery store chain in San Francisco, provides a shuttle that brings customers to and from its stores. The company realized that the very first step—actually getting to the store—was a pain point in deciding whether to shop there in the first place. Had someone not considered the user's *true* starting state when evaluating the effectiveness of the end-to-end customer journey, the store might not have achieved a decrease in total time spent getting groceries and may have had fewer customers as a result.

Obstacles

The last term that we will scrutinize from the definition of *pain point* is *obstacles*. Obstacles represent friction or other difficulties encountered as the user attempts to complete the set of actions required to reach the goal state. We refer to this set of actions as a user journey. One of Jerry's goals is to finish his trip promptly, so obstacles that slow him down are likely to represent pain points.

Once inside Safeway, Jerry first needs to find a cart (which will help him navigate the store more quickly, as well as transport his groceries as he selects them). Once he has his cart and is shopping, he will have to locate an obscure spice (which the store might not carry). Both of these steps could easily turn into pain points if something prevents Jerry from fulfilling them.

Another example of a grocery store pain point:

- **Journey step:** Jerry searches for the ingredients required to make his ham and cheese sandwich.

- **Obstacle:** Ham, cheese, and bread are in three different locations of the store.

- **Pain point:** Jerry spends extra time roaming the store to find the ingredients he needs to make his lunch, potentially jeopardizing his goal of completing his trip in under thirty minutes.

Any step in the journey might have multiple pain points, depending on the user and their goals. As a product manager on the job—or as a PM candidate in an interview—it could be very helpful to map out a user's perceived journey steps in sequential order, noting any possible underlying pain points along the way.

Let's take a quick break from Jerry to discuss two common methods for identifying pain points: **funnels** and **loops.**

Funnels

In a funnel analysis, PMs look at each step in the journey from the starting state to the goal state. The steps represent a (typically) linear set of actions that the user must follow; PMs analyze the user's progression through these actions. Then, we hypothesize where users might feel pain.

A user purchasing Allbirds shoes might take the following journey.

Steps:

1. The user decides that he needs some new shoes for walking (his starting state).

2. He uses Google to search for "comfortable shoes."

3. He clicks on one of the top results, Allbirds, and lands on the company's home page.

4. Finding the value proposition attractive, he clicks to browse Allbirds's latest shoe collection.

5. Upon finding a pair of shoes that he likes, he adds them to his cart.

6. Happy with his choice, he concludes that he's finished shopping for shoes and begins the checkout process.

7. The user adds his shipping address and email address.

8. The site asks the user to create an account or continue as a guest. Which should he choose? The result would create a separate flow with its own subsequent steps. For simplicity's

sake, let's say that he opts not to create an account and will complete his purchase as a guest.

9. Oops, his credit card is in his wallet. He leaves his laptop, retrieves his wallet from another room, takes out the credit card, returns to his laptop, and enters his payment information.

10. He completes his purchase. His new shoes will be on their way soon!

11. He receives an order confirmation, and soon after, a shipping notification.

12. A few days later, the Allbird shoes arrive at his home.

13. He unpacks the shoes and tries them on. They fit! Pretty comfy, too. The user has reached his goal state.

As a PM at Allbirds, your task might be to map out this user funnel and try to improve it. There are steps in this funnel that are pain points, such as whether or not a user should be required to create an account. Points that require the user to input information (possibly personal) add friction. Is the benefit to Allbirds of collecting account information sufficient to outweigh the potentially high number of users that will choose not to enter the information (and possibly leave the site) before completing their purchase? This trade-off would be essential to dig into if optimizing this funnel was a priority.

The data would likely indicate that requiring the user to create an account would increase the amount of time to order completion and potentially have a negative impact on whether or not the user chooses to complete checkout. You might monitor and analyze the data from users passing through the funnel steps (in very granular detail). Where do users "drop off," or exit your user flow? You'd look at drop-offs at each step along with associated metrics, such as average order volume, number of items, et cetera. If you observed that many users failed to finish the credit card step, you'd have identified a potential pain point. How might you relieve or remove it? If you did so, what would the value be to the Allbirds business?

Funnel analysis shines when your user journey is linear. A significant decline between two steps in the funnel represents an opportunity for the PM to hypothesize that a pain point exists.

Additionally, a funnel is a tool that can help your team and organization visualize and understand the user journey. Funnels are not exclusive to Product teams—many other cross-functional teams use the concept of funnels, as well.

One must consider a pain point within the context of the user's goal. In both the grocery store and the Allbirds examples, it may feel natural for us to hypothesize pain points because most of us have been this user before. Funnel analysis goes hand in hand with data analysis. At each step, ask yourself, "What information do I need to measure to most confidently suggest how to improve this experience?"

Furthermore, one shouldn't always analyze funnels by aggregating the behavior of all users at the same time. It's important to remember that different cohorts, personas, and user types will behave differently. Grouping subsets of users with similar characteristics together might yield insights and opportunities to improve the user journey that would otherwise be missed.

Loops

Funnel analysis sometimes falls short when the product exhibits a non-linear user journey. Loops (a repeating series of actions that provide the user with increased value at each turn of the loop), are an alternative way to look at a user journey—especially when the product experience is cyclical and the user accrues value over time. In this section, we will examine several products and look for pain points utilizing the concept of loops. Analyzing a product or an app's loops helps to build product sense, which can be used to build better products, or to have more productive conversations with other PMs, or to stand out to potential interviewers.

Free-to-play games have a concept called the "core loop," which refers to the cycle of basic gameplay that users follow daily or within each session to progress within the game. In *FarmVille*, we called the core loop "PPH" (plot, plant, harvest). The player builds some garden plots, plants seeds in those plots, and returns later to harvest the crops. The player can then sell their harvested crops and plow and plant *more* land; thus, the loop repeats. If that core loop doesn't resonate with our digital farmers, they don't play the game very long. There's strong evidence that this loop works: the *FarmVille* games have retained players for many years and have earned billions of dollars in revenue.

In another space entirely, many B2B SaaS tools try to improve the workflows of other businesses by offering a free version or a free trial in order to attract new users. A prospective customer engages with the product and attempts to establish daily use of their new tool. If enough value emerges during those early sessions the business may become a paying customer.

Let's look at an example. Productboard is a SaaS tool that gives PMs and collaborators a dashboard to aid in core activities such as prioritizing a backlog, planning and tracking releases, and building roadmaps. Its value proposition is compelling to product teams that need to collaborate broadly with other teams as well as with cross-functional partners. Spreadsheets and other conventional processes used by PMs for roadmapping purposes can be suboptimal in terms of their feature sets, difficult for nonengineers to understand, or simply uninspiring or homely in design (we're looking at you, Jira!).

Teams design products with the intent for them to be habit forming. This means that users utilize them over extended periods of time and the user value accumulates as they become more engaged with the offerings. If you were a PM at Productboard and trying to improve the growth and adoption of the platform, think about what you would want users to do. What is the happy path, for first-time users, that leads to the most successful and highest-retaining customers? How does following this path add value each time users traverse it?

1. A user creates a new board on Productboard for a project.

2. A user creates a to-do on the project board.

3. He or she invites other members to the project.

4. They add or update tasks, create new boards, and share the roadmap with the broader team.

In this example, Productboard wants users to follow this loop continuously in order to grow its user base. At the same time, each user is accruing value as he works toward his goal—namely, to execute on a roadmap more efficiently and transparently. Instead of a linear path, the product embeds itself in the user's mind and routine and replaces any existing tools that were previously used to pursue the same purpose.

In the Productboard example, pain points are harder to isolate than they would be for a product that has a clear user funnel, since the experience doesn't follow a linear sequence. The first turn of the loop could be higher converting because it would be a simple test run of the software. Perhaps the user intends to demo Productboard over a period of a few weeks. If the user realizes sufficient value from the tool, one might expect that:

1. Within the user's organization, the number of users with Productboard accounts increases over time.

2. New users are contributing to shared spaces.

3. The number of spaces is increasing over time.

To identify pain points in loop examples, the metrics and data that a PM collects and analyzes for a tool like Productboard might be spaced out over a longer period of time than for an ecommerce or mobile gaming product. You might ask questions, such as:

- What is the retention rate of new users?

- If they join this week, how many return to the product and take some action the following week?

You might also want to look at user engagement (i.e., user activity in the platform over time, as measured by values such as session lengths, actions taken within a session, number of weekly or monthly logins, etc.), and whether that engagement is increasing, decreasing, or remaining approximately constant. Since one of Productboard's value propositions is roadmap transparency, another important question might be whether new users are opting to share their tasks and roadmap with others.

If an obstacle or failure in a specific part of a loop is identified, examining some supporting behavior metrics at each stage of the loop may yield clues as to what pain points might exist, and where.

Back to Jerry

Now that we've defined and deconstructed what a pain point is, and have covered some methods to help identify them, let's return to Jerry and see if we can help improve his experience at the grocery store.

For this experiment, we can assume that Jerry follows a linear user journey. It is also possible to think of the grocery experience as a loop, if we were optimizing for longer-term retention and value gained over multiple visits. However, let's use the funnel approach for now.

In practice, these journey steps would be identified by observing or communicating directly with customers: either through data analysis (of the user's flow through their workflow) or qualitative methods (such as customer interviews or survey results). However, during interviews—or when roughly outlining an idea and demonstrating your empathy for the customer—you can reach a generally acceptable approximation of the user journey.

With Jerry, over the course of his journey through the grocery store (in an attempt to reach his goal state), we can see a series of slowdowns and inefficiencies. To answer the question, "How would you improve the grocery store experience?", we need to apply a structured approach to ordering the steps in the workflow from most to least impactful—a process called "prioritization" that PMs use daily.

For now, how would you decide which of Jerry's pain points to tackle first? Once a pain point is defined, what would you do to mitigate it? Structured approaches to answering and communicating these questions will ultimately help you interview more effectively when looking for your next product job, and to excel in that job. In the next chapter, we will outline prioritization frameworks thoroughly, as they are a foundation you will need to succeed.

CHAPTER 4

How to Prioritize and Maximize Opportunities

The final step in figuring out the "what" in the WSB question, "What should we build and why?" is to identify the most impactful improvement that your team can apply to the product using active, deliberate prioritization. PMs prioritize all phases of product development; however, we believe prioritization is one of the fundamental skills needed in order to answer the WSB. Effectively, each time you form a hypothesis about what needs to be built, you are tapping into amassed knowledge about your customer, or a problem space your customer has encountered, in order to inform that thinking.

As we saw in the last section, even a grocery store can be rife with possible slowdowns, such as disorganization or other obstacles, so it should now go without saying that we can easily brainstorm a meaningful list of pain points. But which issue will we choose to solve?

The reason that PMs prioritize

Let's examine why prioritization is a core PM job responsibility. We've mentioned before that, in every company, there are many highly capable and intelligent individuals who are able to suggest product ideas or improvements and, certainly, many of those ideas can be (and often are) implemented. Prioritization is the step *after* idea generation but *before* execution and it can make or break a product or company's success.

Why? Effective prioritization maximizes impact, minimizes cost to build, and positions the product and organization for success over the longer term. Ranking prospective features to build a product roadmap is both an art and a science. You *could* simply intuitively pick items from a list so that developers and designers always have things to work on and don't sit idle. However, although it might seem easy to use gut feeling and experience in the domain space to decide the feature on which your team will focus next, could you defend your decision if a teammate or a leadership stakeholder were to challenge it?

These methods *might* work, especially if there's a major competitor doing the same thing to whom you can easily point. Increasingly, however, tech companies are placing an emphasis on data-driven or data-informed decision-making. In other words, sound structure. A prioritization framework helps with providing an organized way to select the next step a team should take. Selecting the most *important* features, tasks, or new initiatives likely requires implementing some process and structure. Additionally, such a structure will enable you to more easily change direction when new information becomes available or things don't go as planned.

What's in a Framework?

In order to weigh ideas against one another, we need a method based on a clearly defined set of variables. We will eventually arrive at a decision based on a comparison. A **prioritization framework** is a tool for structured decision-making, allowing a team to distill a complex problem into an enumerated list of solutions, ranked by the impact. We strongly recommend that you learn at least one framework, incorporate it into your own style, and practice applying it to sample case studies before interviewing or starting a new PM job.

Effectively prioritizing a backlog of needed feature improvements requires the following elements:

- Categorizing features (e.g. growth initiative, revenue feature, tech debt, design polish, etc.)

- Measuring potential impact or considering other business value and costs

- Ranking features in order of importance based on the standardized measures (impact, cost, etc.)

Many PMs develop their own methods and frameworks—based on a version of the process above—when managing a backlog or building out a roadmap. A prioritization framework only works when those involved agree that it is the right framework to use. Imagine if our business only accepted dollars while our customers exclusively used euros. In order to successfully transact, we would have to align on a common currency before any business transactions could occur. Thus, you should attain alignment with your stakeholders and leadership early and often on an approach to prioritization.

Calculating return on investment is at the core of prioritization. From an ROI standpoint, the question to ask might be: What improvement can we focus on that will yield the best outcome for the development costs incurred?

Additionally, prioritization frameworks should:

- be applied consistently so that all upcoming items, pain points, or tasks can be judged by the same set of criteria;

- be understandable by those outside the immediate team. Everyone should be able to see the rationale behind a decision (simple frameworks are often better than complex ones);

- take into account all possible impacts to the business, its customers, the number of users, development costs, confidence level, industry climate, and competitors—as well as the urgency to prioritize a given task;

- provide a clearly defined goal, in the form of either a metric the team wants to move or a milestone that the team needs to hit. When everyone is aware of and aligned to the same goal, ranking ideas becomes much easier;

- always account for costs, usually in terms of engineering time (expressed as days, weeks, or possibly in **story points).** It is also important to account for other variables such as design, research, the time of an outside team member—and how all of these will contribute to delivering the final product.

At any given company, prioritization will operate in slightly different ways. The nuances of a particular product or customer type will impact how a team decides what to work on next. High-level guidance still applies here, but the criteria, cadence, and value of the business impact will certainly change from organization to organization.

For example, at a large company like Facebook, it would be a good guess that prioritization is done faster, and with a focus on smaller optimizations. The price of being *wrong* is smaller, since they operate at such a massive scale and are able to iterate quickly. However, the price of being wrong at a healthcare or a hardware company is much larger; therefore, a more thoughtful and longer term approach is often required to avoid making mistakes.

Challenges in prioritization

Prioritization can never be done in a vacuum or by just one person. While prioritizing correctly on a roadmap should follow a logical process, it is also a bit of an art form. The larger the team, the more complexities that can arise. In this section, we are going to list several challenges that a PM might face and how to mitigate them. Perhaps your past experiences will help you to identify with these—and keep in mind that you will likely be asked about times when you successfully overcame a prioritization challenge in your PM interviews.

Handle it like a PM

The urgent request. Executives, salespeople, and other teams or stakeholders will often request that their product-change requests or features be moved to the front of the product development team's queue. At a B2B company, for example, an account rep might receive a feature request directly from a customer and want to get the feature built ASAP in order to unlock additional revenue or earn that client's good graces. A dev team almost certainly already has work of its own, so it can be difficult to say no.

How to mitigate: Show your prioritization method to anyone who comes with a request. Walk through it with them. Try to discern a business and customer value behind the request, and work with them to determine if the request is something that might impact more customers than just the one requesting it. Every feedback, request, or action item should be added to the roadmap and prioritized the same way so that there aren't transparency issues. That said, part of prioritization is knowing what problems *not* to solve, so always keep in mind your goals and what's most important to you.

Losing sight of the bigger picture. It is easy to get bogged down in the day-to-day planning, focusing on smaller feature details or optimizations from the team's backlog. When this happens, the team can lose sight of the overall mission and vision of the team and the company, which can reduce morale and development speed.

How to mitigate: Always spend time reiterating the goal. At least on a monthly cadence, but it doesn't have to be as rigid as that. Put it at the start of every slide deck, or ask people to remind you what it is. Then, using that knowledge of the goal, hold brainstorming sessions for larger, bigger ticket items that might move you closer to that goal. That way, you will have a mix of bigger and smaller items on the roadmap.

Incorrect costing. It can be almost impossible to estimate the development effort required to deliver a big, new feature. If done incorrectly, this leads to missed expectations and team morale diminishes because of potential missed deadlines.

How to mitigate: A lot of upfront work should be done to poke around the new area to figure out what the complexities or blockers could be before doing any work. Define the **minimum viable product (MVP)** as clearly as possible, identify all possible overlaps with other teams or technologies, and add additional time to the roadmap for potential roadblocks ahead of time (often called buffer room) so as to keep things on track and minimize the chance of rushed-out products.

Two examples of prioritization frameworks

Prioritization frameworks are tools that can help you navigate some of the pitfalls we just reviewed. We'd like to introduce you to two frameworks that we chose specifically because they are widely used and demonstrate use of the characteristics of frameworks we previously described. There are many other examples of prioritization frameworks available, but we find these two to be simple, yet effective, when it comes to determining the features that you and your team should build and those you should not.

A prioritization framework is a tool, and it is the right tool for a specific job. Just like a carpenter knows which tools to use in order to build a table, a PM must know which tools to use at each stage of creating a product. You don't want a screwdriver if you need to drive a nail into a wall. Learning a variety of approaches will help a PM tackle many challenges in prioritization.

The following two examples will be great additions to your PM toolbox. As we have stated, there are many more frameworks out there and, on the job, teams often develop their own.

The "Three Feature Buckets" framework

The first framework we'll introduce is the concept of "Three Feature Buckets," written and popularized by Adam Nash, who has served as VP of Product & Growth at Dropbox, CEO of Wealthfront, and VP of Product at Linkedin. He frequently writes about how to be a great product manager and leader on his blog, "Psychohistory." As one of the most influential writers in the product space, his essays have been viewed (at the time of this writing) almost four million times.

One such essay, "Guide to Product Planning: Three Feature Buckets," written in 2009, was the introduction of this framework. In it, Nash states that features for software products should fit into three categories, or buckets:

1. Customer Requests
2. Metric Movers
3. Customer Delight

Customer requests are direct feedback from clients or users on how to improve their experience or make their lives easier through improving the product. It is important to consider such feedback because:

- Customers feel valued when a development team implements their suggestion, which can lead to increased retention.

- The end users are often right, and they are the ones for whom you are trying to create value.

However, customer or user suggestions or requests might not ultimately resolve core issues or pain points. A client may have a perceived solution to a problem she's experiencing but fixing it exactly as she suggests (without fully evaluating the new UX) could mean that the core issue remains unresolved or even that a new one arises. In addition, the PM and development team will need to consider whether the solution will solve similar issues faced by other clients.

Metric movers are features that are built for a specific business outcome, such as increasing subscribers, engagement, or growth. Have you determined and agreed upon the North Star Metrics for your organization or feature area? Teams are often judged by how much they move the needle on certain KPIs that often include metric movers, and it is important to ensure that the team has adequate resources to drive the business forward and improve the product's health. Metric mover features are designed and prioritized to influence user behavior in a certain way—with a clearly defined success metric, usually related to the North Star Metric, or revenue goals in mind.

When metric movers are prioritized and developed, they represent improvements to the product that are measurable and clearly signify that the Product team is using its time and resources effectively. Consequently, metric movers usually represent some significant percentage of an organization's roadmap. Showcasing such wins to leadership can earn the team considerable credibility.

Customer delight is the bucket of features from which users derive value without specifically asking for those features. Delighting the customer often requires a mix of understanding user pain points, solid product sense, awareness of new technologies, and great design sense. This category is important for differentiation in a saturated market, but it can also improve user satisfaction and retention under any circumstances. It is also the hardest bucket to justify, since it doesn't directly translate into revenue or other KPIs at the start, but ignoring this bucket will not be great for the product in the long term.

How to use this framework: Categorizing your backlogged features is the first step in prioritizing. By doing so, you are adding some structure to your process. As a team, you'll need to really internalize the "why" of a specific effort, and placing items into buckets is a great first step.

Once you've identified the categories, you'll need to think strategically to determine where to allocate resources. If your company has specific KPI or revenue targets, you might allocate most of your team's time to metric movers. If you are a B2B company and have some high-profile accounts, effectively managing those relationships and fulfilling the customer requests is vital. Customer delight features *should* be incorporated but, especially when encountering stiff competition, you might gain some additional ground by investing in great experiences or other differentiators. With some of the teams that the authors have worked with in the past, we have agreed to allocate some portion of our design and development budget to customer delight, in order to consistently make some progress in that area.

One additional category that deserves mention is **technical debt.** Technical debt is accrued when a change to software is introduced using an imperfect technical approach, with the understanding that it will be reworked later. It is also a category bucket that you would be smart to include. If you ignore technical debt, and continue to pile on more and more "hacks," you will eventually reach limits on the system and each new feature will require more work than the last. It's generally a good idea to balance efforts toward reworking older systems with new user-facing features, so that the product evolves in a harmonious way.

The RICE framework

The RICE framework—made popular by the product team at Intercom —is a simple to use, clear, and effective method for prioritizing competing features.

The framework entails creating a list of potential product changes or improvements that the team is considering and then assigning scores for each of the following criteria:

- *Reach*: How many users or customers does this feature impact?

- *Impact*: What is the impact of implementing this feature?

- *Confidence*: How certain are you of the impact?

- *Effort*: What is the effort required to complete it?

For each of these categories, the PM can assign a numerical score for each feature, and the output is a list of ranked features. So, an item with high impact, high reach, and low cost would likely make it to the very top of the list. However, confidence might impact this as well: if there are many unknowns, the score for that feature would be reduced. Even when there are trade-offs, such as a feature with higher reach versus another with higher impact, it should still be possible to rank priority after factoring all the variables of the framework together.

Look at the example in the table below. At first glance, you can see that Feature B has higher impact, which may lead you to think that is the most important feature to build. However, Feature A requires slightly less effort to build and has stronger reach, which means that focusing efforts here first would maximize the output of the team's work on an ROI basis. In order to calculate the RICE score, the PM multiplies the values in the first three columns (R*I*C) and divides by the value in the final column (E).

	Reach	Impact	Confidence	Effort	Final Score (RIC/E)
Feature A	9	5	6	7	39
Feature B	6	9	5	8	34

The RICE framework is a tool that allows you to optimize and maximize your product roadmap in a world where efficiency is the name of the game. While useful, it's important to note that prioritization is also a bit of an artform and not a hard science. The final score output is helpful for ranking, but as company strategy evolves and new information arises, consider revising the input numbers.

Checking in

At the heart of solving problems like a PM lies an intimate understanding of your users, knowing which obstacles or behaviors you'd like to change, and determining the order of delivery. In this chapter, we examined several simple processes: applying user empathy, identifying customer types, evaluating pain points, and prioritizing.

These are fundamental skills that every PM needs to have and be able to demonstrate in interviews and to the teams that they work with. The process of identifying and delivering impactful value is the most important piece of the entire product development puzzle. The ideas that come out of exercising this skill are the output of the PM's work: creating processes and frameworks to uncover value and that will lead the product and the team to the most fruitful outcome.

This cannot be understated. This is the foundation upon which the PM mindset, and skill set, is formed. These are the building blocks upon which great careers and longevity, anchored on flexibility, are formed. Mastering these fundamentals, and making them your own, will lead you down the road to success as a PM generalist—capable of contributing to Product in any arena.

CHAPTER 5

Execution (Bringing a Product to Market)

"Everything you do on a daily basis—roadmapping meetings, cross-functional collaboration, anything . . . you're the multiplier on awesomeness. Your team can probably do things without a PM: they have engineers who can code, the designer can design, but the end result is not going to be larger than the sum of its parts, so to speak."

—Khalid Ashour, PM at Twitter, former PM at Facebook

Product delivery is the process in which the idea gets iterated on, planned out, and finally built by the engineering and design teams. Once we figure out "why" we need to build something and "what" we will build, executing comprises the "how" that's going to happen.

Managing the successful delivery of a feature is a fundamental PM skill because bringing new experiences to customers and reacting to how they use them is as important as performing adequate problem discovery.

The PM is the catalyst during this end-to-end process. A carefully curated roadmap is only as good as the ability of a team to deliver it; thus, a product manager with a demonstrated track record of successfully releasing features is one of the most desirable candidates among hiring organizations. Often, you will see PM job postings that ask for "experience shipping products 0 to 1," meaning that they are looking for someone to come in and establish their successful execution process—someone who can hit the ground running immediately.

A successful process is learned through repetition, and the more a team delivers features, experiments, or new experiences, the more fine-tuned that process becomes. This chapter focuses on what a process might look like for a team, based on our own experiences in doing just that.

In this product-delivery chapter, we will cover:

- a widely accepted and effective process for a PM to use when delivering features;
- notes on how to manage stakeholders during the execution process;
- the partners with whom a PM typically works from day to day, and what they do;
- how to use data to form KPIs and how metrics play a role in the process.

All about process

Shipping features, from a PM's standpoint, has the potential to become difficult for the simple reason that there are many variables outside of our control.

A PM can't assign delivery dates, foresee bugs in the software, or accelerate the engineers' work. With all of these reasons to feel like you've got your hands tied behind your back, how *does* a PM fit into the execution process? Delivery and execution, from the PMs perspective, boils down to a few key responsibilities.

- Ensuring that all feature ideas, as well as customer needs (often called requirements), are documented and prioritized

- Working with engineers to solve any potential blockers to development

- Collaborating with other development teams or PMs to ensure any overlaps are understood

- Keeping the rest of the organization aware of progress

- Determining the success metrics or KPIs the product team should be tracking

- Managing the release of the feature and creating a go-to-market strategy

- Creating a backlog of prioritized improvements

Obviously, this is a nonexhaustive list, because depending on the industry, team, or product, plans and schedules can go in a million different directions. It should go without saying that, rather than robotically executing the delivery of features and products, a PM should understand how to effectively deconstruct *why* a specific process is currently inefficient and suggest new ideas that catalyze improvement.

In an interview scenario, you will likely be asked to describe how you built something end to end. The interviewer will not only want to hear about the finished product but also what you did to continually improve the execution process all along the way.

To illustrate a nice end-to-end process, let's look at the life cycle of a feature. The following sections demonstrate something of an aggregated version of what we have been involved with across our experiences working at tech companies in the Bay Area, LA, and NYC, as well as working with development teams globally.

Phases of Product Development

Building features follows a fairly consistent life cycle that is agnostic to the organization in which you're working.

Whether you are at a brand new startup, or a giant company that has been building products for a long time, the stages and steps to deliver a quality feature don't change much. Different organizations may take slightly altered approaches to any given product or feature development, but in this case let's assume that we are observing a product development team of sufficient maturity to be deliberate about how, when, and what is being built.

Phase 1: Identify a Product Gap, User Pain Point, or Experiment

A product change or feature is typically first conceived as a response to some gap in the product, such as a customer need that isn't being met or an optimization that is identified based on data. We previously covered the key points of prioritization, but let's list a few here as a refresher:

- **Competitive analysis:** Something that a competitor's product has and your product does not.

- **Customer/user feedback:** Comments or complaints as indicated through interaction with your customer support staff, app or product reviews, or ad hoc comments.

- **Employee feedback:** Sometimes, some of your best ideas and constructive criticism can come from fellow employees who are working on or using your product. Ignore them at your peril!

- **Leadership:** Executives or corporate board members may also have ideas for how to improve the product. These may be friendly suggestions or imperatives that you will need to incorporate into your roadmap.

- **Product team expertise:** Your product team are the people who know the product most intimately and also have the most specialized expertise: design, engineering, data science, and product. These folks, over time, should develop some intuitive understanding of where the product should go as it evolves.

Phase 2: Initial Concept

This step is the PM's chance to justify an identified feature or product change and why it should be built. In some companies, a deliverable created by a PM for this purpose might be called a "one-pager." This is a summary of the discovery work that has been done in order to identify the feature. Whether or not it is a single page, it should be relatively brief and give some context for:

1. the problem the organization is trying to solve;

2. how the feature/change might solve said problem;

3. what the basic scope of the feature/change would be;

4. what product metrics the PM expects to move with the feature improvement and by how much.

Amazon asks its PMs to create mock press releases during this stage of product development and pitch them to a large group of collaborators and stakeholders. Whatever your organization's method, this is an opportunity for a PM to articulate her vision, argue the merits of what she wants to build, and make a case for it.

Additionally, it's an opportune time to find alignment, at a high level, on overall direction. If you're creating a ratings-and-review system in your product, do you intend to build the entire feature in-house or potentially partner with a vendor to help with the heavy lifting? This is not a bad time to start such conversations.

Phase 3: Research, Exploration, and Validation

Once the one-pager has been presented, debated, and finalized, it's time to do some heavy lifting with respect to the problem at hand. If you're lucky enough to have a UX designer and/or researcher on staff, this would be a great time to employ them for a week or two, to better define the problem and the approach to solving it. The PM devises the problem statement and goals, and partners with a designer to help further flesh out what a new experience might look like. To do so, the team should employ formal and informal research methods.

Some techniques that would be appropriate at this stage could be:

- Surveys

- User interviews
- Prototyping and observation of user interactions
- Audit of your company's existing product or UX flows

All of the information gathered via the methods listed above will help increase the likelihood that your team is building the right thing in the right way.

Phase 4: Detailed Product Requirements

This is the real meat of the PM's documentation work.

After alignment has been achieved and initial research has been completed, it's up to the PM to get down to the work of defining exactly what the feature will look like and how it will function. At this point the product manager will enter a period of deep collaboration with others on the team, most directly their engineering partner and perhaps a design partner (for a user-facing feature). Additionally, the PM will likely consult other stakeholders in the organization, such as product analysts, sales or marketing colleagues, CRM, QA, or others.

The PM should document these conversations in order to, ultimately, give the team guidance on what to build. In some organizations, or for certain types of features, this guidance might be a long-form document that describes the work that the team will do. Such documents are commonly called "**specs**" or "**PRDs**" (short for specifications, and product requirement documents, respectively).

We've seen a number of formats for these types of documents, but most often they are created with Word/Google Docs or PowerPoint/ Google Slides. It's really up to each product organization, or even the individual PM, to decide how best to organize and communicate the information necessary to bring a feature to life.

A spec is a great mechanism which is used to ensure that a PM has spoken to all of the people with whom she'll be working—to denote how the team will proceed and to provide a single source of truth— even if, ultimately, the PM only uses it only for her own reference. Whether the PM, a project manager/producer, or an engineer ultimately translates the spec into individual tasks that engineers and designers will work through to ultimately build the feature, it's immeasurably helpful to have created something in advance that will give a complete picture of the vision.

Some might argue that PRDs or specs run counter to **agile methodology** and more closely resemble **waterfall development**. We disagree. More than anything, the spec is a roadmap for a particular feature that serves as a starting point and helps the team to stay within scope, avoid distractions, and give the full complexity of the solution due consideration—so that it can be built efficiently and as close to what was imagined as possible.

There are almost always pitfalls and new learnings during the development stage, when the team will slightly (or more than slightly) shift course and make design or functional changes.

A spec format that might be a good starting point could resemble the following (if any of these terms are unfamiliar to you, refer to the glossary near the end of the book):

1. Feature title
2. Overview, goals, and success criteria

3. Planning:
   a. Feature size (Small, Medium, Large, Extra Large)
   b. Feature owners (Product, Analytics, Design, Engineering, etc.)
4. High-level feature description
5. Purpose and context
6. KPIs/Goals
7. Feature details, such as
   a. UX flow
   b. Verbal description of details
   c. Wireframes/mockups
   d. Feature surfacing points
   e. Edge cases
   f. **Acceptance criteria**
   g. Any other information that makers and stakeholders should know before the feature is built
8. Experimentation: Planning for any A/B testing around the features
9. Additional technical requirements or considerations
10. Analytics and data requirements
11. Open questions
12. Release plan
13. Future considerations
14. Competitive research appendix

The sequence above roughly resembles the format that we've used at several organizations that we have been involved with, but a PM might add, subtract, or reorder based on her own needs or those of her employer.

Phase 5: Development

After the spec has been written, debated, and fully fleshed out—including **edge cases** and **wireframes**—the PM works with the rest of his team to translate the feature into tasks that will be assigned based on skill sets and interests. At this point, it's the job of the PM to help the team adhere as closely as possible to the agreed-upon template for the feature, as well as to make adjustments as new information and opportunities come to light.

Of course, testing is a massively important part of the development process. If you're lucky enough to work with a QA or testing team, you will have very meticulous and dedicated support in this phase. If not, think about how you can enlist others to help you try to "break" the product before you ship. We firmly believe it's the responsibility of everyone on a product development team to ensure that high-quality code, design, and user experience are introduced to the live environment from the start, but this is doubly true for the PM. For better or worse, the PM owns the outcome of the release and will bear the brunt of any negative feedback from inside or outside the company if something goes wrong.

Do whatever you have to do to see and interact with the feature in a test environment before it's shipped. Give yourself ample time to explore every nook and cranny of the build. The time and effort that you invest now—especially if you catch some easily identifiable bugs while they can still be corrected (and before users encounter them)—will give you peace of mind and save you headaches and heartaches later!

Phase 6: Release

Going to market is the exciting part!

Your release is live and you can finally see the results of all of your hard work, out in the wild. Whether you actually pull the trigger yourself (via some sort of feature toggle or admin tool), or an engineer does the deed via deployment, it's an important milestone for your team that everyone can celebrate and be proud of.

A few points to remember as you approach this moment. As the PM, you will want to work with any customer-facing or marketing teams to ensure that they are aware of the feature and that a clear plan for how the customers will actually get access to it is available. This information should be provided in something called a **go-to-market ("GTM") Plan**. These can come in many forms and are less prescriptive than specs. There are many questions you may want to ask yourself as you prepare for a release, the answers to which you may want to include in the GTM Plan.

- Is all of your testing complete and have you addressed any critical bugs?

- Have you spoken with all of the relevant internal and external stakeholders? Do they know what's coming and have they had adequate time to prepare?

- Are there any blockers for the release that need to be solved before you flip the switch?

- Are you communicating this change to your users? If so, how? (Make sure any push notifications, in-app messages, or emails have already been sent or are ready to go out.)

- How are you planning to measure success or report that to your teammates?

- This may also be the time to enable any experiments you may have decided to include when rolling out the feature.

The most important part about GTM Plans is that everyone in the organization has seen them, has signed off, and is aware of any timelines they outline. Creating these documents falls on the PM's plate but requires a significant amount of input from many different teams such as marketing, sales, support, and leadership.

One of the most exciting aspects of being a product manager comes after you have built something with your team and have observed how it is used out in the wild. No matter where you work, members of a high-functioning team will inherently look for their next steps. A PM's role is to highlight what those new opportunities could be and why they should make their way into your newly-released product or feature's roadmap. Even after a major release, the PM is on a never-ending quest to answer, "What should we build and why?"

Stakeholders: Invested in the Success

We've just discussed the phases that a product or feature would go through during development, but building features is not the only thing a PM needs to do during the execution. During the process of building anything in a tech company, you will need to manage input from a significant number of other individuals, and thus managing stakeholders is a key part of the job.

A **stakeholder** is a person with a vested interest in your project. Those who are investing in its success will have viewpoints on the direction the project should take, and at times you may need to fold their goals and plans into your own before you can move to the next phase. As a PM, you might have several (or even many) different stakeholders within your orbit.

Managing internal stakeholders is a crucial part of the PM role. Because of this, you can count on fielding many questions related to stakeholder scenarios in the interviews you will face during your job hunt. Stakeholder empathy will be vital as you navigate these challenging behavioral questions.

Stakeholder management is the process of thoughtfully aligning with the company leaders, clients, and others who may have a stake in the product—through the building of an understanding of their motivations and goals—to develop a "common currency" with which to bargain, and a common ground on which to stand and discuss ideas.

Who you will need to work with and how you will manage those relationships will differ dramatically depending on your company size, industry, maturity, and a million other things. However, the principles of stakeholder management apply in almost all cases. For example, if you are at a smaller startup, the total number of people you will need to influence or otherwise work with will be smaller than if you are part of a large, public tech company. That said, the weight of these fewer relationships will be much higher (i.e., you can't escape them in the office if things go south).

To have a productive conversation and make progress, both parties need to speak in the same terms. It's the product manager's job to identify and facilitate a shared understanding. Through the rest of this chapter, we will examine just how product managers achieve this.

A cross-functional scenario

A prevalent type of friction that can occur between the product and engineering teams is technical debt. Technical debt, as a refresher, means that the team knowingly implemented an imperfect functional design to expedite its delivery. In some situations, perfect is the enemy of good. Engineering is responsible for not only the birth of a feature but also the quality of the code and scalability of the design. They may be concerned about the fact that the team will have to go back and rework the result of this technical debt later. A scenario that might occur could be that the engineering team wants to double back and tackle old technical debt while the PM wants to innovate on new initiatives.

Management Strategy: Share the backlog. Allow for longer-term planning around strategic goals, which will enable engineering foresight into which pieces of tech debt they will focus on (and when), as well as easier balancing of product goals and timelines. Ensure that some percentage of time is dedicated to reducing accumulated technical debt.

Cross-Functional Collaborators

A factor that can impact, influence, and cause fluctuation in a product manager's day-to-day life is the composition of her immediate team. PMs need to wear many hats and those hats are sometimes determined (at least in part) by their peers. Product managers often can't do very much without their teammates (especially designers and engineers). Your goal as a PM is to be a facilitator and/or a multiplier of your cross-functional partners' efforts. PMs have considerable opportunity to interact with many other teams and contributors—often across the scope of the entire business—so it is helpful to have a holistic understanding of these folks and their roles.

- **Engineers/software developers:** These are usually a PM's closest partners. Sometimes referred to as "makers," it's difficult to build and maintain a digital product without people who can actually write and deploy code. Engineers (stereotypically) love to work through tough challenges and are great problem solvers. Often, they appreciate that a product manager can help them to understand what to build, why to build it, and when, because they may not otherwise be inclined to work on features that would be most impactful to the business or user experience.

- **Designers:** Designers are another set of makers. These folks work with product managers and engineers to craft a user experience for a feature; work with other designers to share patterns for the user interfaces; and collaborate with the PM and engineering to determine the best solution to a problem: all through the lens of usability and intuitiveness. Some function as distinct UX designers, others as visual designers, and still others hold artist roles, depending on the needs of one's organization.

- **Quality assurance:** QA associates are an incredibly valuable part of a product development pod. Although everyone on the team should consider themselves responsible for delivering high-quality results and identifying bugs, QA literally does this full time. They often know the specifics of the product better than anyone (sometimes to the embarrassment of their PMs!). Today's QA professionals are increasingly technical and may even have the ability to automate aspects of testing.

- **Product marketers:** Product marketers often "embed" with Product teams and specialize in areas such as making go-to-market plans, planning advertising and user-acquisition campaigns, implementing **SEO** and **ASO**, managing customer relationships, and ensuring brand development and adherence. A great product marketing partner can help grow the product very aggressively, while keeping it aligned with the company or product vision.

- **Product analysts:** These team members can deliver the deepest insights about user behavior as illustrated through product usage and metrics. Although we believe that most PMs should develop their own abilities to access data (in whatever environment they happen to be operating), the business intelligence team is often the best fit for particularly complex or deep analyses that might go beyond the grasp of those who lack their expertise.

- **Program/project managers:** Most product managers will have some degree of project management inherent to their roles. However, a program or project manager can often play this part much more effectively through specialization and focus. Great project managers "see the Matrix" when staring at a board full of Jira tickets and are experts at keeping the team moving forward, enforcing deadlines, and managing dependencies both within and across teams. When a PM is lucky enough to have a project or program manager supporting his team, it can allow the PM to focus on strategy, research, and longer-term thinking about the product roadmap. In media, entertainment, and games, project managers are referred to as "producers."

Contention Between Disciplines (Peter)

While various team members will ideally work in perfect lockstep unity, I've also been in situations in which this was not the case. One example of potential friction between teams might occur when both Sales and Product clash on prioritization.

The relationship between those two teams can be both symbiotic and problematic, sometimes even contentious, especially at tech companies. The Sales team is in direct contact with the customer and, thus, has firsthand information about what a client might need. This type of information is what product managers need in order to ship better features, but PMs aren't as readily in touch with the end user.

Now, while Product is looking to find a solution that solves problems for many customers at once, and has more knowledge of how this can happen (from a technical perspective), Sales might know that a certain feature is clogging up productivity for a select number of customers. If the feature bug that Sales has identified is fixed, that customer cohort will be free to use the product more fully, increasing revenue. However, what if this is not Product's priority? Such a disagreement can lead to a clash over the issues at hand and continued friction down the road. Sales can't order the Engineering team to develop a feature, and the PM can't order Sales to keep her "in the know" with the latest customer intel. Some might liken the relationship between Product and Sales to a marriage: when it becomes rocky it can lead to conflict, animosity, and even a dysfunctional organization.

Managing Up

Managing across is a term that describes the relationships you cultivate with the members that make up your team and the other teams you interact with, also known as your cross-functional pod. These peers consist of the collaborators and partners we just outlined. *Managing up* is how you communicate your vision, progress, and plans to those who sponsor your initiatives with their executive support and resources. In other words, the leadership. Sometimes these folks are called executive sponsors, other times they may be VPs and directors, but regardless of their titles they are a core group of stakeholders with whom you need to empathize.

To manage up, you need to zoom out and take a higher-level view of your initiative. What does your product or feature mean for the business? Does it drive revenue, or strategically position the company against its competitors?

Directors, and those above them, will want to know how your project is going to improve the business overall. As the PM, it will be your responsibility to provide this information. Knowing how to effectively demonstrate to them the potential trade-offs or how to request finalization on any strategic decision points—and, ultimately, empathizing with the tough, but impactful, choices that they often must make—will go a long way when presenting to execs.

KPIs & Analysis

Data is the key to understanding how a product is performing. It's an important step throughout the process, and a mechanism critical to finding important problems to solve, or to measure against once you have solved them.

Product managers are a select breed that, by definition, should be paying the most attention to user-behavior data. In other words, the product metrics or KPIs are a core responsibility for PMs to track, analyze, interpret, and ultimately communicate to everyone else.

Because PMs are expected to have a deep understanding of user needs and pain points, and to also have the ability to analyze and interpret data, they are ideally positioned to draw conclusions from such data and identify and prioritize how the product could be better.

Data is also frequently and consistently used in discovery—when deciding what to build and why—to analyze customer pain points, validate strategies, or identify feature gaps. It is absolutely essential when creating roadmaps and optimizing user experience.

Gathering data

In almost every instance, your product will have some kind of tracking tool that will help you understand your users and their behavior in the product. Some organizations build out their own tracking and data infrastructure; great examples of this are the big dogs of tech, including Google, Facebook, Amazon, and Netflix. More commonly, small startups might use an off-the-shelf product such as Mixpanel, Amplitude, Google Analytics, Looker, or another SaaS alternative. PMs in some organizations might query their databases directly using SQL (a coding language used to manipulate data from a database). Usually, however, this is more directly the domain of data scientists and product analysts. There are companies where PMs need more data-querying skills, but it's not too difficult to learn these skills in just a few weeks of practice nor is it generally a deal-breaker during the hiring process.

A core part of collecting data is to first understand the questions you want to ask. A mistake that many PMs make is to list out different metrics that they want to know, without fully understanding how they will be used later. If the planning for how the metrics will be used comes too late in the process, you might have difficulty completing a meaningful analysis of your feature's impact.

It's easier—and ultimately more effective—to frame analysis questions in plain English. Rather than say "I'd like to know the

ARPDAU for users in the lowest monthly engagement bucket," you could simply say, "How likely are our least engaged users to buy?" Try not to overcomplicate, and be sure to ask and document these questions early on. You can further define them when execution nears completion or you are about to rigorously analyze the data. In an interview context, it is permissible to be ignorant of the exact KPIs for a product (although it certainly doesn't hurt) but, if you can, show that you understand the customer behavior that the metrics represent.

Experimentation

Running experiments is another tool that PMs use to answer data questions as they relate to analysis.

An experiment is a way to help optimize specific parts of the product or software experience. For example, if a PM is not quite sure what pricing to set for a specific bundle of products, she may explore two different price points using an A/B test—with users randomly assigned into a group for each price point. The results may indicate which pricing yields the highest conversion, or the most total revenue per user.

When designing or proposing an experiment, it's very important to be mindful of the questions you are asking and what the expected result may be. Very often, PMs or stakeholders will ask to run an experiment whose results may not be actionable or without clear goals. Developing these tests pulls engineers away from other assignments, so it is prudent to run an experiment only if you truly have a specific outcome in mind. *The Lean Startup* summarizes it best. "As you consider building your own minimum viable product, let this simple rule suffice: remove any feature, process, or effort that does not contribute directly to the learning you seek." Author Eric Ries is not suggesting that you forgo running experiments; rather, he is advising you to be aware of what you are trying to learn about your customer, and to focus on only that.

> **Braxton Sidebar:** Near the end of my time at Zynga in 2015, I was in a room with several executives who were considering various growth proposals—to quickly understand whether they would find traction and, if so, build more robust teams that could turn them into hit games or initiatives that would earn the company tens of millions of dollars or more. The meeting was an hour long. Over the course of that hour, multiple stakeholders shared their ideas and, after a few minutes of discussion, someone would say "We should test that!" and we'd move on.
>
> By my count, at the end of the hour, we had brainstormed at least a year's worth of experiments, most of which would go nowhere. What I realized was that many senior-level folks have never worked on a product directly and don't realize the effort that goes into not only experiment planning, but also design, development, testing, rollout, and then waiting for the results to reach statistical significance. (And oh, *by the way,* some experiments NEVER reach statistical significance, because the differences in user behavior between the two or more variants are not all that different OR you've placed your experiment somewhere in your product that not enough

people will be exposed to it!). A single experiment can take months or more to execute, depending on these factors.

Over my next few PM jobs, this was a pattern I saw repeated again and again. I learned to try to take shortcuts by leveraging the increasingly available results published by PMs elsewhere or finding a similar UX pattern repeated across similar products at massive scale (like Amazon, Facebook, or Google). There's no reason for a small startup or even a larger company to try to reinvent the wheel on certain concepts in 2021.

If A/B testing comes up in your interviews, an understanding of the difficulty of execution and measurement associated with experimentation—and the wisdom to choose only those experiments that really, really may answer questions to which you don't know the answers—will help differentiate you from someone who only knows basic experimentation theory.

The KPI acronyms

Sometimes, we like to use the metaphor of product managers as "doctors" for their products, because PMs are so deeply attuned to the normal ranges of common metrics that they know what a healthy or unhealthy product looks like. Some example metrics are:

- **DAU:** Daily Active Users, or the total number of people who use your product on a given day.

- **ARPDAU:** Average Revenue Per Daily Active User, or how much revenue an average user brings in on a given day.

- **Retention**: The number of users who return after X number of days (after one day, two days, seven days, fifty days, etc.).

- **Engagement**: How much use (including frequency) an average user gets out of a product in a given time period. Commonly abbreviated as DAU/WAU or DAU/MAU, which stands for daily, weekly, or monthly active users.

- Other metrics specific to your product, perhaps a "North Star" such as daily orders, rides (Uber), or turns *(Words with Friends)*.

Over time, a PM will learn to innately understand how these metrics move—by day of week; over various business cycles; or after major events, sales, campaigns, or promotions. The metrics will move up and down, similar to how our heart rate, blood sugar, cholesterol, body temperature, and other vitals exhibit variability under different conditions. In a given product, some of that movement may be inherent to normal function, while other movements may be indicators of a buggy release or a feature that isn't performing as expected (in which case the PM's "patient" might be sick). For a bad feature, it might even be necessary to amputate. It's essential that you make hard choices, as needed, to help your product survive and ultimately thrive.

An example of a feature that was "amputated" would be the group dating feature in Tinder. Tinder, a mobile dating app, was primarily used for one-to-one connections. However, at one point they added a way for users to organize group dates. This feature was eventually removed. Can you think of some reasons why?

Perhaps Tinder noticed a decrease in total matches, or number of messages sent per user. If so, they may have hypothesized that group-dating follow through was too intimidating. Furthermore, they may have run a test or had a holdout group, and noticed that overall user engagement dropped once the feature was released to the users. Ultimately, it might be fair to hypothesize that Tinder users didn't want to group date, or were less likely to find a partner successfully when that feature existed in the platform.

It's important to understand the normal ranges for your product's metrics, but it will inevitably be necessary to go deeper. You'll search for answers not only when something goes wrong, but when considering how you can structure a roadmap intended to improve weaker parts of your user experience, or double down on some of your product's strongest characteristics.

Identifying important metrics

You must learn to quickly formulate analysis questions when examining products. It should become second nature to quantify how customers behave, in either a product that you are working on or one that you are auditing. Think about this as a three-step-funnel: **acquisition, activation, conversion.**

- **Acquisition**: How are customers arriving at the start of your product or feature? Where are they coming from? Are they coming through specific channels? (SEO, paid, organic, etc.) It's important to understand how your customers are entering the product for the first time, as they may be entering from different angles, or from various entry points within the product (when trying a new feature, for instance).

- **Activation**: A user may become activated through a variety of methods, and this is generally when they fully start to experience the product or feature. For example, activation may have officially occurred after they have signed up, or made a post, or created a group. Activation is the step that requires the most critical thinking by the PM: what does it mean for the customer to "use" the product and how might you measure that? As well, what are the associated metrics that demonstrate "how" they are using it?

- **Conversion**: This is the step in the funnel that signals that the user has received the value they wanted, and then converted in some way. Converting can mean a number of things, such as purchasing something, retaining for a long period of time, or inviting a friend. Along with the actual percentage of users converting, it's also important to think about the secondary metrics: How big was the purchase? How frequently do purchases occur? How long does it take to complete a transaction (from the time the user begins putting items in his cart to the time of successful checkout)?

All of these points should be food for thought when thinking about metrics as they relate to a product you are analyzing. You want to remain thoughtful and curious about the ways users interact with features. Not only do you want to know the data behind the behavior, you will consider how to use that information to inform what to do next, or what you might change to make the user experience more efficient.

When you interview for a PM position, the concept of metrics will certainly come up. In product execution interview questions, you will be asked to evaluate trade-offs between metrics. Which metrics do you consider more important than others? Which metrics are **counter metrics** (that signal when a feature is not working as intended)?

Always refer back to your strategy, vision, and North Star success metrics. The key to effectively using data as a PM is to use it to guide your product toward the goal that you, and the company, have set.

CHAPTER 6

Do You Know Your PM Superpower?

So far in Part 1 of *Product Sense,* we have highlighted how effective product managers can distill a high-level and ambiguous question into a beautifully delivered product or feature. These concepts, which serve PMs well on the job, will also benefit you greatly in your interviews, during which you will be expected to articulate and demonstrate your knowledge and understanding of them. We're going to transition into learning about how to get the PM job, but first, as a checkpoint, we're going to help you articulate your unique PM strengths.

As you have probably noticed, there are many different aspects to being a PM, and no PM is going to be excellent in all areas. You will not be expected to be a magician. Hiring managers will want to hire you because you possess a unique blend of skills that cannot be found in other candidates—often, to balance out a team or because they think that your talents will deliver important value and missing out on you will be a loss for them. We call this blend of talents your *PM Superpower,* and you should learn to craft and rehearse it so that you can easily be recognized as a top-tier candidate.

Developing Your Superpower

Organizations will decide—based on your story and how well your skills translate to their open PM roles—whether you can add value.

Your mission throughout the interview process, starting from the moment that you apply, will be to convince them of your value. Your unique experiences, strengths, and passions will ultimately help you define and articulate the superpower that you bring to bear in product management. Your superpower is the central thesis of the narrative that you will use when persuading an employer that *not* hiring you would be a mistake, and that you will not just facilitate product development but multiply their current impact tenfold.

To hone, prepare, and ultimately demonstrate your unique skill set and traits, you will:

- Use your narrative and superpower to sell yourself when asked why you want the job;

- Consider your strengths and identify and pursue roles that give you the best chance at succeeding;

- Exude self-awareness of your superpower, which will help you focus on areas of interest during your interview preparation;

- Craft a career story that highlights your successes and what led you to where you are today ("Tell me about yourself . . .").

Ensuring that your superpower is properly framed will necessitate drawing clear connections to the skills and responsibilities that great PMs possess in abundance—the common denominators of successful product management that are shared across companies and industries.

If you haven't taken time to reflect on your strengths, don't worry: we've created a self-assessment that will help you catalog the areas in which you shine (as well as areas where you might need to do some polishing). You'll use this knowledge throughout the rest of the book. Pay close attention to where you need some study and practice, and where you can use the interview frameworks as a lens to focus your own experiences.

Common PM Traits and Skills

On the one hand, there are hiring teams that are on the lookout for a PM with a certain specialty or domain expertise. On the other hand, there are general fundamentals that all PMs need to demonstrate.

The following pages highlight the general skills that hiring managers look for, and that well-rounded PM generalists need to have. We based these fundamentals on our collective experience working in product for many years, in combination with knowledge gleaned from the PM leaders who contributed to this book, as well as the dutiful consolidation of literature created by Product thought leaders since the inception of the role.

To conclude Part 1 of *Product Sense*, we've created an assessment to help you understand your own abilities in the context of the PM role and interview process.

How to use the assessment:

You can download a PDF of the assessment from our website (productsensebook.com/superpower); or, if you prefer, you can build your own spreadsheet or document on your computer and fill it in as you go.

In the table, the fundamental skills are listed vertically (each with its own row), while the columns give you space to evaluate them. The second column provides a brief description of what each skill represents. Let's look at the remaining three columns:

- **Passion**: Which fundamental skill (or skills) are you most passionate about? Do you want to be able to do more of this in your next job? Would you be excited to have this fundamental in your daily life? To determine your level of passion for each fundamental, pick a number from one to five, one being "least excited" and five being "most excited," and add it to each row in this column.

- **Skill**: How confident are you in your ability to successfully utilize this fundamental skill in the workplace? Could you demonstrate your aptitude in this area if asked to do so during an interview? In this column, please answer with one of the five options listed here:
  a. This is new to me.
  b. I don't know if I've done this.
  c. I have some ability here.
  d. I'm confident I can do this.
  e. I excel in this area.

- In the last column, describe or map out a scenario or a story from your work history (or personal life) that demonstrates your use of this fundamental in some way.

PM Self-Assessment of Fundamental Skills and Experience

You can download a PDF of this self-assessment from our website at productsensebook.com/superpower.

Fundamental Skill	Brief Description	Passion	Skill	Point of Experience
Discovery stage	Conducting user research, creating a competitive analysis, identifying pain points			
Prioritization	Evaluating trade-offs, identifying MVPs, and making decisions			
Building strategy	Crafting the vision, analyzing market trends, evaluating competition			
Cross-functional leadership	Managing relationships, appropriate communication, giving presentations			
Project management	Releasing a product or feature, resolving blockers, effective roadmapping			
Analysis & KPIs	Analyzing data, optimizing values, defining success			

Your Product Superpower

As a PM, your superpower isn't a single skill that makes you great. It's the culmination of your passions, strengths, and individual experience. It's what makes you stand out. You can't (or shouldn't) make the claim that you are good at everything; but your self-assessment will help you to internalize, and demonstrate, your unique value. It will help you to confidently navigate the "Tell me about yourself," and "Why are we talking today?" interview questions. Your best value from the assessment will be to turn your results into a story—a story that calls out clearly what your PM superpower is.

Using Your Self-Assessment to Develop Your Superpower

1. From your results, pick the top one or two areas that you are most passionate about.

2. Then pick the top two or three skills in terms of how well you know them.

3. Finally, pick a top skill and develop an experience or story that demonstrates it.

Guess what! You now have what you need to concoct your elevator pitch! To begin, highlight what you are most passionate about.

- *"What inspires me every day is the thoughtful discovery of user needs through conducting interviews and determining their biggest pain points."*

- *"I am a data nerd, and can spend hours in front of spreadsheets developing pricing models."*

From here, build onto this with your strengths.

- *"My passion for analytics guided me to a data-driven approach to product strategy."*

- *"I developed a system for organizing user stories for maximum efficiency, as well as forging strong relationships with engineering partners to develop things on time."*

Wrap it up with a story that demonstrates your skills and strengths. This way you cover all the bases: what you are passionate about and how that matches the job role, what you are good at, plus an anecdote that shows how they all tie together.

It's always important to be introspective about your personal strengths and goals. You also want to make sure that once you start applying to jobs, you are applying to the right ones—considering both fit and overall passion. Remember how we talked about finding the North Star, and the right vision for a product? When you are interviewing, *you* are the product. Do you know what you want to work on, and what you would be good at? Making a change in a career is about finding this fit, so that you not only get the job but stay happy in your new role and hopefully work, grow, and evolve in it for a long while.

You will likely be asked why you want to work at the interviewer's company, or what would make hiring you a good fit. Knowing your superpower will give you the confidence you need to demonstrate that you are on the right path.

Going Forward

In the next section of *Product Sense,* we will apply what we've discussed thus far directly to product case questions, which are the types of questions you are likely to face in a tech company interview.

However, self-assessment is an essential first step. In the back of your mind, you should know which strengths you intend to focus on and the areas that you believe stand out based on your initial self-evaluation. Remember that you can always refer back to these chapters as you start to practice for your interviews. Also, many of the terms we have called out throughout this text are in the back of the book in our easy-reference glossary.

The first step toward interviewing as a great PM is being a great PM. You already have your product sense, and we hope you developed or refreshed your understanding of the fundamentals. The next step is to apply these concepts in an interview setting. Internalizing and strengthening the fundamentals outlined in Part 1 will make your interview practice (and ultimately your interviews) that much more effective—and lead to better results.

PART 2

Acing the Product Management Interview

CHAPTER 7

PM Interviews

Welcome to the next step on your journey, where you take your Product problem-solving skills and use them to get your next PM job.

So far in *Product Sense*, we've dissected the component pieces of the existential PM problem statement, "What should we build and why?" When applying for jobs, the interviewers want to hire someone who will effectively confront this challenge. Any question you're going to face in the interview during recruitment will be some variation of this problem statement. WSB is what PMs need to solve in all cases, and the reason why organizations need to hire PMs in the first place.

Therefore, thorough knowledge of the WSB concepts we outlined earlier will help you deliver the quality answers companies are seeking (which is why we covered them first). As we have stated from the beginning, Part 1 of this book isn't meant to be an all encompassing view of the PM role, but it *is* meant to give sufficient breadth of the discipline so that you can show your ability to tackle the WSB problem. Now it's time to apply this knowledge to your PM interviews. The guidance below will help you become a legendary PM candidate.

Here's a high-level overview of Part 2:

1. General context on what PM interviews entail, and why they are consistent across product teams.

2. What the common types of PM interview questions are, with examples.

3. An overview of the Compass Framework, how it was designed, and how to use it to effectively answer case questions.

4. Some example questions (and our responses) that demonstrate the Compass Framework.

Let's get started!

Introducing Rahul

As PM career coaches, we have guided many current and aspiring PMs through the process of securing a new job.

Rahul, an energetic and entrepreneurial PM at a SaaS company, had been working behind the scenes building out APIs and data-related features for several years. He had started to feel his career growing stagnant, and his company was on its third round of layoffs. Furthermore, he felt worn down from building internal systems and features that only benefited his other PMs and their engineering teams; it seemed prudent for him to look for a new job. He set his sights on moving to a smaller consumer-tech company, so he could build features that directly impacted users, and feel closer to his entrepreneurial dreams.

Right off the bat, Rahul dove into navigating his opportunities and started taking interviews. To his dismay, he had generally negative results. He was often rejected after an initial conversation with the hiring manager, perhaps due to his nervousness when asked to share his thoughts on different products. Rahul sought help to improve his interview performance and found his way to our coaching services.

We discussed Rahul's interview experiences with him, and helped him to pinpoint the questions that tripped him up, such as: *"I want you to tell me about a product that you use every day. What makes it successful?"* The interviewers always probed further after his initial answers, *"How would you improve it? What would you tell the developers to do differently?"*

What left Rahul confused after each interview was that he thought he had given great answers pertaining to the products he likes, as well as very innovative new feature ideas. Nevertheless, he wasn't getting called back. We hypothesized that he was jumping too quickly into his ideas for new features, without fully demonstrating the line of thinking that led those ideas. In other words, he was establishing the "what" (he knew what to build), but he was missing the "why" (why his improvements would make the product better). We showed Rahul how to adapt more of a structured approach in his answers, one that clearly showed his train of thought. Using our techniques, he was able to secure a job at a fast growing car-sharing startup—a PM position that was in line with where he wanted to be in his career.

Product manager interviews are more about the why than the what

You may think you know your favorite product like the back of your hand and that you could list ways to improve it without hesitation. However, as we saw with Rahul, diving too quickly into that list can be like shooting yourself in the foot.

The truth behind these interview questions is that the interviewer doesn't actually care about what you come up with (the product you choose or even what you like about it). What an interviewer is looking for in this instance is the process: a structured process in which you lead them to a coherent answer. Early in your interviews for a PM position, you will be asked to verbally dissect and improve various products so that the interviewer can determine if you understand the concepts behind the answers you give. In order to help you accomplish this task, let's go through this process piece by piece.

To start, we will highlight a series of product case questions you should expect to be asked, and explore why companies include them when interviewing. We will then outline strategies to help you answer these questions confidently and thoroughly. To accomplish this we will introduce the Compass Framework, which we have designed to make answering product case questions easy. This framework builds directly on the WSB problem and concepts.

What Will They Ask?

Generally speaking, most companies ask their PM candidates fairly similar types of interview questions. Familiarizing yourself with the style of these questions, and knowing why they are asked, will allow you to walk into your interview with the highest level of confidence.

If you were to be invited to an onsite interview at a FAANG company (and these companies are known for conducting very predictable PM interviews) you would likely be faced with three case interviews, each tackling a different aspect of product management. As we have mentioned before, **FAANG** is an acronym that refers to

Facebook, Amazon, Apple, Netflix, and Google. These giant tech companies hire PMs and engineers on a constant basis. To be consistent in their hiring, they typically follow the interview protocol we are outlining in this book, as do many other tech companies of equivalent size.

There are four PM interview categories that the big-tech companies generally adhere to. They are (along with a brief definition of each):

- Product Sense and Design (how you think about designing products)

- Execution (how you would manage and operate an existing product)

- Product Strategy (how you would define a high-level product strategy)

- Leadership (how you would manage relationships with your peers, within your team, across cross-functional teams, and with stakeholders)

These interview categories have been adopted by tech companies across the United States, as well as tech hubs across the world. In an interview setting, they provide a baseline for the PM candidate's ability. The task of screening the wrong candidates out (and the right ones in) follows a formula of its own. In order to hire PMs at the scale of Facebook, Google, or any of the other FAANG behemoths, the interviewers themselves have been **calibrated**. This means that the company placed *them* into an interviewer-training program and coached them to conduct interviews according to a certain criteria (which includes the four categories listed above), all before ever sitting across from you in a PM interview. The advantage here is that, with most of the big tech companies following this method, it ensures that similar questions will be asked, and a consistent grading process will be followed. For example, Zynga's strict protocol and training process for PM interviewers involves conducting practice interviews, as well as shadowing several live interviews.

Another example of interviewer calibration comes from a FAANG-sized, cloud SaaS company, where interviewers have been trained to cover around nine or ten different question categories in their PM interviews. As they maneuver the candidate through each of these categories, the interviewers are required to ask the exact same question. Any deviation from this protocol risks hiring a PM that doesn't adhere to the company's rigid PM persona. Companies train people to select from these categories so that the content of the interviews (and scoring rubrics) won't differ from other instances.

At Google, in addition to sometimes asking estimation questions (i.e., "How many manholes are in New York City?"), technical (coding) questions are often on the agenda in PM interviews. The culture at Google is such that PMs, as a day-to-day responsibility, must be able to debate technical trade-offs with members of the engineering team and possibly other stakeholders. This is where Google has set the bar for their product teams; thus, they must confirm a candidate's level of coding knowledge to ensure that they hire more technical PMs. This book won't cover in detail how to answer estimation or technical questions. If you anticipate being tested on your technical knowledge during your PM interview, we would encourage you to research online for available resources on these topics. We can say that the technical questions you might be asked will certainly be less rigorous than those faced by candidates seeking engineering positions.

The examples above give an overview of how the larger companies typically strive to hire PM generalists. Companies like Facebook, Google, and Amazon look for PMs with solid fundamentals that will adhere to their baseline product principles. These PMs could find a home on many different teams within such large-scale organizations. Hiring generalists allows these companies to retain good talent longer, since there is considerable openness to internal lateral movement, as well as a shared understanding that cultivates a sound Product culture.

So is it possible to know what a company might test you on in advance of your interview? In a word: YES. If you ask, recruiters will most likely give you tips on what to expect, as they are incentivized for you to land the job. They want you to succeed, so don't be afraid to ask.

You can often find examples of previously used interview questions if you do a little research on Glassdoor, where current employees (and prospective candidates) post reviews, salary information, and interview intelligence pertaining to many major tech companies. Another source is Blind, which is an anonymous forum where verified professionals discuss their current company climate as well as interview formats and questions.

What are the common denominators between the companies we've discussed and how they hire PMs?

In researching this book, we surveyed dozens of PM candidates who had interviewed with companies such as Airbnb, Google, Facebook,

Microsoft, and Adobe. Those companies usually supply candidates with written rubrics to help them prepare and know what to expect from the interviews and how they will be judged. From those rubrics, we identified the interviewing patterns and questions you are most likely to encounter in your next PM interview. Our research also revealed that many startups are now staffed by former FAANG employees, and therefore, those startups have adopted interviewing and hiring processes on par with the biggest companies. So, whether you are aiming for a FAANG company or a startup, this section will help you to properly prepare for your interview.

The Four Types of Interview Case Questions

A PM case question is an interview question that poses a scenario or problem for the candidate to solve using his or her product knowledge and learned skills. The questions may be broken down into four categories. We touched on these categories previously in this chapter, but now we'll examine each one more closely.

1. Product Sense and Design
2. Execution
3. Product Strategy
4. Leadership

Your understanding of these concepts will be useful when we discuss the framework required to answer them. Let's start by looking at what each represents. Then, we'll take you through how to answer them using our Compass Framework.

1. Product Sense and Design: Demonstrating That You Understand the Fundamentals of Building Products

Product sense questions probe for your ability to think critically about products in various contexts, articulate why things are (or should be) built in a certain way, and consider the outcomes or behaviors the product is trying to drive based on the design choices made. Many times these questions will point to how you might design a particular system related to the company's product lines. Other times, your interviewer might ask you to analyze a hypothetical scenario that attempts to push you outside of your comfort zone. The fundamentals mentioned in Chapter 3's discussion of user empathy, in Part 1 of this book, should serve as a guide for the kinds of skills you will want to demonstrate when answering these questions.

It just so happens we have already primed you with an example of a product sense scenario when we covered problems and pain points. You may recall Jerry and his trip to the grocery store. We didn't choose this scenario out of thin air; it was an illustration of an actual product case question that is very consistently used in PM interviews. This question has also been known to pop up in interviews at FAANG companies.

The following is a sample of this common type of product case question:

> *"Let's say that you lead product management for AMC Theatres. How would you improve the in-person cinema experience?"*

Why is this a common interview question? Let's think about it from the interviewer's perspective:

- **It is purposely ambiguous.** The candidate must find a way to apply structure to a large problem space.

- **There are many possible solution paths.** Whether Jerry goes to the grocery store or the movie theater, there are many possible problems he may encounter; therefore, there are many opportunities for solutions that will help him avoid or solve these problems.

- **Measurable success.** Each solution path can yield a KPI for measuring customers' successes in the store.

- **Wide range of concepts tested**. From pain points and goals to user journeys and prioritization frameworks: the ideal answer should touch on a number of these.

Providing structure in ambiguous situations is a core responsibility of the product management role. In turn, product-sense questions are designed to tease out that part of you.

Other real-life examples of product sense questions include:

- What is your favorite product and why? How would you improve it?

- How would you design an app to help friends plan travel together?

- What would you change about Uber to lower prices?

- If Facebook wanted to enter the hospitality market, how would you design that product?

2. Execution: Showing That You Understand Product Metrics and KPIs

Product execution questions challenge your understanding of the important KPIs and metrics for a given product, often through a scenario that a PM might face on the job. Execution questions are about navigating the day-to-day product operations of a live product. Demonstrating an understanding of trade-offs and how to make a well-reasoned and confidently articulated plan for the team to execute is key. If product sense and design involve conceptualizing something new, then product execution is optimizing what already exists—with an understanding of how users are behaving in relation to a current feature.

Execution questions generally have two flavors:

1. **Something happened**. The interviewer wants you to investigate a change in the metrics and formulate an action plan.

2. **Trade-off evaluation.** The interviewer asks you to choose between two or more feature options. How do you make your choice?

Here is a sample question:

"You make a change and it increases the average YouTube-video viewing time, but it also increases the app-loading time. Do you launch the feature?"

This question asks you to analyze a scenario in which there are two possible options: increase the viewing time (at a cost of longer app loading), or maintain your current viewing time with faster app loading. The interviewer wants to know where you would start, given such an ambiguous challenge. This type of product execution question is basically a "metrics brainstorm." Can you tell, by evaluating data, when products are doing well or not? What would you do to change or influence the metrics? And so on.

Remember, the question that PMs always face is "What should we build and why?" Reacting to changes in the product and validating those changes with data is part of answering this question. What are your hypotheses for the changes in metrics? Why are these changes important for the product team to pay attention to? Based on the hypothesized metrics, what would you build or change?

Other product execution interview questions:

- Netflix customers are not renewing their subscriptions as much as they used to. What is your plan?

- What goals or success metrics would you use if you were in charge of Facebook Dating?

- A new feature causes NYTimes.com's articles to load five percent slower, but also increases the number of articles visited by five percent. Do you keep the feature?

A good way to prepare for this part of your interview is to research the KPIs of your target company ahead of time. Do a product audit and make a list of the KPIs you identify, and any possible questions that come to mind. Pay attention to the Acquisition, Activation,

Conversion (Remember these from Chapter 6?), and Retention categories and jot down a few KPIs for each one. Speaking about these metrics with confidence will show that you have a natural analytical mind, as well as some domain knowledge of the space.

3. Product Strategy: Can You Develop a Product Strategy for the Business?

Product strategy questions are meant to be thought provoking because they ask you to stretch beyond the typical PM day-to-day deliverables. This is your chance to demonstrate that you can see the bigger picture and highlight what the business needs are—not only right now, but in terms of how they will potentially evolve over time. Strategy is just that: goals for the future and big bets on how to achieve them. Remember, as we talked about in Part 1, strategy comes from an overall vision, so identifying and understanding the product vision will be an important part of your preparation.

Here are some sample questions:

- Should Facebook enter the insurance business?

- What can Reddit do to make more revenue from its users?

- What can Uber do to differentiate itself from its competitors?

- What should Twitter do to enter the e-commerce space?

- What can DoorDash do to win in the food delivery industry?

Your goal here is not to consider the pain points and prioritize incremental improvements. On the contrary, the examples above challenge a prospective PM to consider the strategic themes in which the company should invest.

One thing to note is that the more senior you become in the product team, the more your visibility into the leadership team and overall business and strategy operations will increase. While much of a company's strategic planning happens at the C-suite and director level, Product generally has a seat at the table. If you apply for senior, lead, or principal PM roles, you will certainly engage in discussions about where to take the business with respect to industry headwinds and the competition. Effectively discussing strategy takes practice, especially if you have been focused on features thus far in your PM career. You should take time to learn to think at a higher level without focusing on specifics before you begin interviewing.

To prepare properly, do your research on the competitors, think of potential unexplored verticals for your target company, and consider what the potential current business challenges might be (such as, they aren't currently profitable, etc.). Tackling these questions is similar to answering product sense and design questions: frame the problem, establish a clear goal, and structure your answer accordingly. Instead of getting into solutions, use the Compass Framework to establish direction or a hypothesis for what would make a solid plan over the next one to two years, or longer.

4. Product Leadership: Can You Lead Without Authority?

The last category of PM interview questions is centered on a behavioral challenge that highlights your leadership, communication, and other soft skills. These questions tend to be less formulaic, since there are many ways to assess these skills. In this area of questioning, the interviewer needs to assess how you might manage conflict or interact with higher-level executives and also determine what lengths you might take to have your project succeed. Product managers don't typically have direct reports to whom they can delegate work, so they must be able to manage the interconnecting disciplines themselves and know how to drive toward alignment.

Here are some sample questions:

- You are a product manager working on a business-critical feature. The engineering team is saying it will be ready in a month, but your marketing manager wants the feature to go live right now. What do you do?

- Tell me about a time you had to pitch for resources to complete a project.

- How do you balance technical debt with feature improvements?

- Tell me about a time that you had to mediate a conflict between two people.

Leadership questions will reveal your ability to follow through on a project and deliver a product or feature. How will you navigate roadblocks, ask for resources, and manage expectations? A PM's work is central to all sorts of different teams and partners, and it's natural for a company to want to know how you would perform under certain scenarios. It would be wise to think of some times when you have stepped up, defused a situation, or saved the day so that you can describe them in detail and with confidence.

Variations on a theme

Of course, not every interview question will fit nicely into these four buckets. Deviations will occur across companies and industries.

Nevertheless, the core concepts and values of product management—thinking about products, determining how to build them, and knowing how to lead without authority—will certainly be tested during your interview process. *What should we build and why?*

When preparing yourself, thoroughly considering these categories to ensure that you can discuss great examples from your professional experience, as well speak to any hypothesized scenarios, will help you feel confident that you are ready for the real thing.

Now that you are aware of *what* is going to be asked, let's next go into *how* to answer these questions using the Compass Framework.

CHAPTER 8

The Compass Framework

You should prepare for each of the PM interview questions—product sense, execution, strategy, and leadership—by practicing them in advance. A framework can guide your thought process and allow you to craft thoughtful responses. Mastering a sound technique will allow you to wield it effectively in a live interview setting.

If you have done any internet research in this area, then you know that there are a handful of frameworks available to help you answer product interview questions. While these can be useful for some, we feel that they are rarely as encompassing as they should be. None seem to lead an interviewee to adequately cover all the concepts and touchpoints that an interviewer is looking for. You want to stand out among your fellow candidates, not blend in with them. If you don't employ a framework that helps you to cover key elements in a thoughtful way, you might end up sounding rehearsed or rigid. This is not the time for a one-size-fits-all formula. You want to demonstrate that you possess the critical thinking skills and mindset of a well-rounded PM.

Part of why we wrote *Product Sense* was to provide a holistic tool for PM candidates to use when tackling product case questions, regardless of the question type. It's not about memorizing a different answering method for each case question but, rather, you want to effectively relay your fundamental PM skills while ensuring that you are hitting the key points your interviewer will be listening for. With this in mind, we designed a framework that is flexible enough to be applied to any product case question and comprehensive enough to allow you to showcase your PM superpowers. We call our method the "Compass Framework."

The Compass Framework: how we designed our holistic approach

Before we delve into the specifics of the Compass Framework, it's important to note the process that we took in creating it. In short, the Compass Framework was designed to take the concepts from "What should we build and why?" and cross-references them with the criteria of how PM interviewers grade their candidates. When we coach PMs, and in our own interviewing experiences, we have found that using this framework as your guidepost for weaving your WSB understanding and knowledge into your answers is the key to demonstrating that you have what it takes to thrive in a PM role. The Compass Framework empowers you to show your interviewer that you will not lose your way in any type of Product quandary or situation: from the day to day, to the bigger picture.

WSB Problem + Interview Grading Rubric = Compass Framework

An aggregate of interview-grading rubrics

Companies are often very transparent about their grading requirements, at a high level. Your recruiter may show you a rubric, and it is also perfectly acceptable for you to ask what a product team is looking for. We were able to gather many of these from tech firms of various industries, and aggregate their common trends. A generally applicable version of a PM-interview-process rubric is shown below, which was used in developing the Compass Framework.

Interview Rubric Categories	Details
Problem Framing and Goal Setting	Can you take a product or company goal and fully outline and understand the context before diving into a solution? Can you identify the key metrics that will indicate success or failure?
Structured Thinking	Can you thrive in ambiguity—set up a framework for analysis, ask clarifying questions, and demonstrate ease and comfort—while engaging in conversation in front of a whiteboard?
User Empathy	How well can you understand the steps a user would take while using a feature or product? Can you identify the likely pain points, and how to fix them? This category also includes the user experience and design aspects of product management.
Domain Knowledge	Do you have relevant previous experience, such as working with engineers and/or domain knowledge? For PMs, "being technical" often means understanding the KPIs and data points that are used for the product category (daily active users, retention, etc.).
Prioritization	Can you effectively weigh one idea against another? What is your process for doing so?
Cross-Functional Leadership	Do you possess the knowledge and poise to adeptly navigate a web of cross-functional partners, as well as the ownership mentality to take a problem and see it over the finish line?
Culture Fit	How well will you fit into the culture of the company? (Google calls this "Googliness.")

As a basis for the Compass Framework, this table summarizes the majority of key rubric criteria. However, PM-hiring criteria often depend on and vary by the specific role, company stage, and needs of the individual team. Discuss the specifics ad nauseam with the recruiter, check out Glassdoor, and stalk the company's PMs on Linkedin. Although criteria may sometimes change, we expect that the broad strokes within these rubrics will endure as long as PMs still exist in the world.

Introducing the Compass Framework

After working through the aggregate interview rubric, we wanted to map these characteristics to concepts from the WSB problem. Recall the concepts we outlined and went through from Part 1, which each had their own time in the sun from Chapters 2 through 5.

1. Vision, North Star Metric, Strategy
2. Discovering User Value, Problems to Solve
3. Prioritization
4. Execution

The Compass Framework is a five-step tool, which takes these concepts, and guides you to internalize, organize, and present your responses to the PM interview questions you will face.

The five steps of the Compass Framework are:

1. Outline a Vision and Identify the North Star Metric
2. Highlight the Strategic Themes
3. Explore Relevant Personas or Cohorts
4. Illustrate With User Journeys and Expose Pain Points
5. Provide a Solution Design

Following these steps when answering an interview question will convey your thoughtfulness, product sense, and mastery of structured thinking. Confidently working your way to a solution (or solutions), while engaging your interviewer in discussion, will help you stand out as a top candidate. Your solutions will demonstrate their weight and importance *because,* once you reach them, you will have proven along the way that you can thoughtfully consider levers to move the North Star Metric that will result in the greatest benefit to the company.

Note that the *Solution Design* step—which may at first seem to be the crux of the interviewer's question (i.e., "How would you improve 'XYZ' product?")—is intentionally placed at the *end* of the Compass Framework's five-step process.

Why? As has been a central theme in *Product Sense,* framing the problem statement and understanding user needs must come before any solution is settled on. We can't stress it enough: *these initial steps are the most important part of the PM job.*

An important note: Alignment

The Compass Framework, as applied during a case interview, should also be viewed as an *alignment* exercise during which you will engage your interviewer. The best replies to an interview question (i.e., the ones that get people jobs), involve collaborating with the interviewer. Your interviewer may interject with their own opinions, direct your thoughts, or ask probing questions. The benefit of the Compass Framework is that it allows you to control the dialog in a structured way. Think of each step in the framework as a milestone. Once you and your interviewer align at Step 1 (Outline Vision and North Star Metric) then you can go to Step 2 (Highlight Strategic Themes).

In other words, agreement with your thought process at a high level is your cue to move to the next step in the Compass Framework. You will essentially be "bringing them down to your level" as you lead them through your thought process, and eventually to your endpoint in the Solution Design step. As we've said, demonstrating your thought process is more important than designing a great solution on the spot. The Compass Framework begins at the broadest level (Vision) and ends with the most acute action (Solution). This type of approach resonates with those working in a product development environment.

If, at each step, you sense that you are heading in the right direction (based on your interviewer's reactions and comments), then when you arrive at a solution or decision, while your interviewer my or may not agree with your assertion, they will at least understand the train of thought that you used to get there.

For example, by following the five steps above, you will end with an important statement which we discussed way back in Chapter 1, when we looked at how to frame the WSB problem.

We are building [Solution] in order to solve [Pain Point] for [Persona]. This is important for the business because [Strategic theme] and [Vision], and will be measured by [North Star].

This is a confident statement and (if each of the steps in the framework were discussed and aligned along the way with your interviewer) the basis of a great response.

Next, let's look at the steps of the Compass Framework in relation to the rubric categories they cover—we want to touch on every aspect that interviewers look for so that you'll leave nothing out of your answer. By now we hope that the Compass Framework is starting to feel familiar to you; it should, since it entails applying concepts from the WSB problem. We hope that you can see how applicable and versatile it will be to you—not only in your interviews, but also in your role as a PM.

Deep Dive on the Compass Framework Steps

For each Compass Framework step, we will highlight how to structure an answer to a PM interview question as well as how to adjust each answer for a specific question type. We will also provide examples that show how each step builds on the previous step, so you can see how a complete answer would flow through the framework. In this chapter, we'll use a design-type question as our sample, followed by some highlights to consider if you were instead faced with an execution-type question.

In the next chapter, we will walk you through six example questions (of varying types) and their appropriate responses. Following all of this we will apply the framework across all four question types, taking a close look at each, so you can experience the framework in action multiple times. Our hope is to give you a very strong feel for how the framework can be applied to any type of case question and to simultaneously help you internalize its mechanics so you can draw from it when needed!

1. Outline a Vision and Identify the North Star Metric

Rubric Categories: Problem Framing and Goal Setting, Structured Thinking, Culture Fit

When you are asked a case question in an interview (similar to making actual decisions as a PM), it is imperative that you articulate the goals for the product, and the company, prior to suggesting anything further. Thus, your first step in using the Compass Framework is to state the *Vision* of the company and determine a *North Star.*

Once you have concretely laid the context for the problem, you will then demonstrate your knowledge of the first rubric category to be touched on (in this case, *Problem Framing and Goal Setting)* by outlining and reaching agreement with the interviewer on overarching goals for the product. As a reminder from Part 1, a North Star Metric is a guiding metric for the *company,* so you must relay that you understand the driving purpose behind the company *as well as* the product and also how success might be measured by leadership.

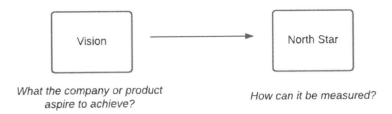

| Vision | → | North Star |

What the company or product
aspire to achieve?

How can it be measured?

- Facebook is connecting the world → *Measured by meaningful time spent on Facebook*

- *Clash of Clans* is easy to learn but difficult to master → *Which you can tell by newly acquired users coming back in a week (D7 retention)*

- Amazon is the comprehensive digital storefront → *Customers continue to come back and have a high average **lifetime value (LTV)***

After hearing the question, you should pause and let the interviewer know that you'd like to first discuss the higher-level objectives. Your interviewer will mentally check off the *Structured Thinking* category, because you've already started to tackle the problem in an organized manner.

To make space for a clear articulation of the vision, you might say something along these lines:

- "Let's take a step back."

- "I'd like to first frame the problem by looking at the goals."

- "With any product improvement, the first step is to understand what we are trying to achieve."

By clearly articulating the high-level vision of the company, you are demonstrating your passion for the product and why it exists; thus, exhibiting *Culture Fit*, another rubric category.

Let's illustrate where this stage of the Compass Framework with an example:

Step 1: Outline a Vision and Identify the North Star Metric	
Company	Music-streaming service
Vision	The world is better with more music in it.
North Star Metric	Songs streamed

Once you've conveyed a vision and North Star Metric to your interviewer, it's time to move on.

2. Highlight Strategic Themes

Rubric Category: Domain Knowledge

After stating the vision and determining the North Star, your next step is to highlight your interpretation of the company's product strategy as it relates to the vision.

If the vision reflects a company's higher-level intentions, then the strategy represents a credible path that the company should take in order to realize these goals. A company creates "strategic themes" when there are multiple strategic areas that can, collectively, represent a high-level action plan on which teams can execute. Strong product teams invest in themes, not features, and when answering interview questions it is important to outline your interpretation of the company's strategic themes.

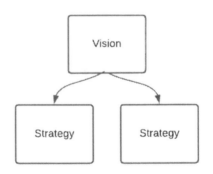

"In order to achieve this vision, the company is employing the following strategies"

Touching on, and aligning to, strategic themes during your interview allows you to accentuate your *Domain Knowledge*. It demonstrates that you are well researched in the space and understand the underlying business upon which the product was built.

Product managers can sometimes become lost in the technology and optimization of product features and lose focus of the business impact of their work. Highlighting your understanding of why products are being built in a certain way will establish your credibility—especially since your interviewer will likely be a senior Product leader. More senior leaders must be more strategic on a day-to-day basis. Demonstrating a strategic mindset will separate you from any entry-level candidates.

There are three types of strategic themes, let's take a look at each one:

- **Competitive developments** are features or projects that the company takes on in order to differentiate against a competitor, or match parity offerings in order to meet market needs.

- **Business goals** are initiatives that ensure that the company is healthy and sustainable (for example: growth, profitability, product habit formation, etc.).

- **Consumer tastes and preferences** represent the development a product undertakes in order to meet a new industry need or customer trend—to avoid stagnation relative to the needs of the market.

Think of these themes as buckets that you continually fill with strategic comments as you navigate the conversation. This will allow you to further demonstrate your domain knowledge of the company and product, and further align with your interviewer, as you scope down the question into more manageable pieces. Remember, you are trying to align with them incrementally about the framing of the problem before getting into the solutions.

Our example, continued from Step 1:

Step 1: Outline a Vision and Identify the North Star Metric	
Company	Music-streaming service
Vision	The world is better with more music in it.
North Star Metric	Songs streamed
Step 2: Highlight Strategic Themes	
Strategic Themes	• Provide all music available for free on the streaming platform (Competitive Developments) • Keep listeners engaged with personalized recommendations (Business Goals) • Allow for easy sharing and social playlists (Business Goals)

The first strategy is classified as competitive development because this condition must be met in order for the company to be successful in this market—most other streaming platforms have almost all music available for streaming, so any newcomer must be at parity. The second two strategies imply business goals, engagement, and growth.

To recap: vision sets the stage, the North Star Metric defines success, and strategic themes define the path. You've articulated the "Why" and, in the subsequent steps, will outline the "What" and "How."

3. Explore Relevant Personas or Cohorts

Rubric Categories: User Empathy, Problem Framing and Goal Setting, Domain Knowledge

The next step toward a solution to your interviewer's question is to identify the users, customers, or personas involved. Here, you can further highlight your *Domain Knowledge* and *Problem Framing and Goal Setting* abilities. What you will identify and clarify, utilizing this part of the Compass Framework, is that you are cognizant of the different user segments that might exist for a given product.

It's important to consider the context of the question you are asked when you apply this part of the framework. Your approaches may vary considerably. Consider the questions listed next to each case type below. Each shows you the perspective from which you can identify several personas and weave them into your ongoing interview discussion.

- **Product Design and Sense:** For whom are you building? What are the user types?

- **Product Execution:** What are the possible cohorts or user segments by which you'd slice and dice the data? Examples might include engagement buckets or LTV tiers.

- **Product Strategy:** How big are the target audiences for each strategic option? What are their switching costs or best alternatives?

- **Product Leadership:** Who are the actors in the scenario, and what are their motivations and goals?

You generally want to call out at least two different personas during this step. This is your first major opportunity in the framework to begin to demonstrate *User Empathy* as you define the personas, their needs, and how the product might help them achieve those needs. Next, you should weigh the various personas against each other, in a structured way, in order to quantify the impact.

One way to do this for Product Design questions is to think about what the impact would be if you were to "choose" to build for the persona's segment. Think about what their goals are, how that persona group is currently being served (by this product or others), and what the relative size of the group is. You might lay this out in a table like the one below. Your criteria and columns will vary, but your goal in this step is to express that, "We are building for this person because of X,Y, and Z."

	Goals	Currently Served	Reach
[Persona name]	What are these persona's goals?	How are they currently being served?	How many people does this persona group have?

This is where your research into the company's product and any competitor products will come in handy. If you can succinctly state what the incumbent competitor does poorly and how you can build a feature or product that better addresses that need for a certain user group (or better yet, all users!), your answer will be much stronger.

When solving product execution questions, which follow the same format, the goal is to demonstrate your knowledge of a product's internal metrics. You might begin thinking about personas, which are hypothetical user narratives, instead of cohorts. Remember from Part 1 that cohorts are a set of users grouped together because they share a specific trait such as geographic location, date joined, engagement behavior, etc.

If you are told that "Your product's daily active users dropped by five percent," you would start by proposing some initial reactions, such as: honing in on low-engagement users, or investigating whether users who installed more than thirty days ago are more or less represented in the cohort of lapsed users. Remember, you're setting the stage for further analysis; if you don't provide this context up front, you won't be able to transition smoothly.

	Reason for Inclusion	Impact
Cohort Group	What are the types of users you want to segment against?	What is the impact on each type of user if the product issue is solved?

Notice above in the table that we listed *Impact* as one of the criteria. The reason for this is to further help clarify the rest of the analysis you'll complete for an execution question. Let's consider a brief example:

> Imagine that the DAU of your freemium product declined by five percent. During your investigation, you wanted to separate paid users and nonpaying users in order to see if one group drove more of the decline. You might notice that the decline in users was almost entirely nonpaying users. Depending on your product, this might be less impactful to the business—because nonpaying users don't directly generate meaningful revenue—and it would also inform any further data analysis because it's now more clear from which cohort you're bleeding DAU. Meaning, you might evaluate a broken new user flow or whether some key acquisition source of these users was underperforming (such as an ad campaign). On the other hand, if the drop in DAU was the result of a decline in paying users, you may take the direction of changing the price, evaluating longer trial offers, or increasing benefits to the paid-subscriber tier.

To summarize where we are at this point in the interview, you have set the stage and framed the problem by stepping back to look at the vision and strategy. You are well on your way to figuring out what to do based on the "Who" and will soon follow with the "Why" and the "What."

Our example, continued from Step 2:

Step 1: Outline a Vision and Identify the North Star Metric	
Company	Music-streaming service
Vision	The world is better with more music in it.
North Star Metric	Songs streamed
Step 2: Highlight Strategic Themes	
Strategic Themes	• Provide all music available for free on the streaming platform (Competitive Developments) • Keep listeners engaged with personalized recommendations (Business Goals) • Allow for easy sharing and social playlists (Business Goals)
Step 3: Explore Relevant Personas or Cohorts	
Personas or Cohorts	• Exerciser • Office Worker • Host (entertainer)

4. User Journey and Pain Points

Rubric Categories: User Empathy, Culture Fit

Now that you have framed the problem by identifying goals and customer persona groups, you can start designing some kind of solution. In the last step, you came to a conclusion (and aligned with the interviewer) about the users for whom you are building. Now you'll take a step further and figure out what to build. You can also use this section to demonstrate *Culture Fit*, since many organizations codify in their values that focus on the customer or delivering customer value is central to their missions. If this is the case for your target company, don't waste this opportunity!

Think back to the chapter on finding the user value, and the concept of user journeys. In a product design interview question, you'll need to outline the steps that your chosen customer Persona would take in order to achieve their goals (the ones that you identified). As you describe each step of the journey, you'll mark or cite one or more potential pain points that would exist at that point, and then move along to the next step. Taking a visual approach, ideally by writing the paint points on a whiteboard as you discuss them, will help keep the scenario you are describing organized. This will also help you to revisit them once you have analyzed each step of the user journey.

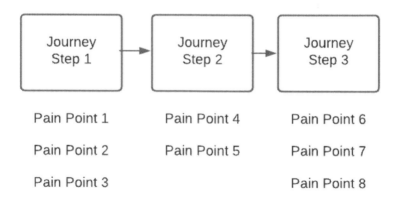

Remember that pain points are great opportunities for you to add value to a product, as they represent areas for improvement. You may have just been asked how you might improve a given product, and now that you know for whom you are making the improvements, you can prioritize the handful of pain points that you have identified. How would you decide which of these opportunities to pursue?

This process is quintessential product management and you'll want to demonstrate that you have the ability to do it confidently. Since you have already established how you would measure success in Step 1, the Vision and North Star Metric step, you can now try to rank these pain points on how impactful they would be for improving the metrics that you and your interviewer aligned on. In addition, you should structure your prioritization of these pain points further by incorporating other metrics or evaluation criteria. This helps drive the point home that the selected path is the most impactful one. The table below illustrates this point:

	North Star	Magnitude	Confidence
Pain Point #1	Show each pain point's impact to the North Star Metric defined at the start.	How big is the impact? How are you quantifying it?	How confident are you that your solution will impact the key metric?
Pain Point #2			

Our example, continued from Step 3:

Step 1: Outline a Vision and Identify the North Star Metric	
Company	Music-streaming service
Vision	The world is better with more music in it.
North Star Metric	Songs streamed
Step 2: Highlight Strategic Themes	
Strategic Themes	• Provide all music available for free on the streaming platform (Competitive Developments) • Keep listeners engaged with personalized recommendations (Business Goals)

	• Allow for easy sharing and social playlists (Business Goals)
Steps 3 & 4: Explore Relevant Personas or Cohorts and and User Journey and Pain Points	
Personas or Cohorts	• Exerciser - Pain Point: Don't want to have to manipulate their music many times during a session - Impact: More songs streamed, higher weekly retention • Office Worker - Pain Point: Recommendations must not be too distracting from work - Impact: Longer sessions, more songs streamed • Host (entertainer) - Pain Point: Continuous music in the same vibe or genre - Impact: Higher weekly retention

In the abstract, we have tried to rank each of the pain points using the following criteria:

- Does the resolution of each pain point impact our North Star Metric?

- How much impact can we drive?

- How confident are we that we can achieve our goal (or is this a complete unknown)?

In reality, you wouldn't structure your prioritization table the exact same way each time. In reality, a prioritization table wouldn't be structured the same way each time. In your interview you will have to demonstrate your prioritization logic in the moment, based on your research prior to the interview, and the direction the discussion is going thus far. In many cases, you might not need a perfect approach; rather, you want to demonstrate a structured process and that you are capable of collaborating with your interviewer when she has feedback.

During product execution questions, you would think about the user journeys in a similar way but, instead of identifying pain points, you would consider which metrics you'd need to know or want to investigate at each step. It is important to think about your metrics in a structured way. One simple way to do so is by thinking about your *Acquisition, Activation,* and *Conversion* user journey steps in a product funnel—a step-by-step flow that mimics what a user would go through on the way to their goal.

For example, if you were asked what to do if you noticed that average order volume had declined in an e-commerce site, instead of jumping straight to purchase metrics, you should first identify and list the metrics that reside at the top of the funnel, followed by the metrics that might be included in the purchasing steps, then finally the ones that happen at the point of purchase (or slightly after).

E-commerce execution journey:

- **Acquisition:** New users, returning users

- **Activation:** Added to cart, number of items viewed

- **Conversion:** Purchased, average item value, repeat purchases

You can see that despite execution and design questions being somewhat different beasts, they can be approached similarly within the Compass Framework. Design questions are about identifying opportunities based on user pain points; and execution is about measuring, optimizing, and evaluating trade-offs for existing products and features. During an execution exercise, you need to propose the set of information and data required to outline next steps.

Trade-offs are an important call out here. When you have a trade-off, it means that two metrics or concepts are competing against each other, and it's up to you to prioritize the more important one. This is key for execution questions because your interviewer will likely quiz you on why the metric you chose is the best one for the business.

Your interviewer may or may not help you by providing more context to the question, but you can and should continue your investigation even without complete clarity. With the information you have, you will be identifying which metrics are important and what they reveal about what the users are doing.

At this point in the framework you have articulated the company's vision, outlined their strategies to achieve it (measured by a North Star Metric, which you have identified), and described the users for whom you are designing and what problems you want to solve for them.

5. Provide a Solution Design

Rubric Categories: Prioritization, Cross-Functional Leadership

In the final step, you'll suggest product improvements or provide clear recommendations to the interviewer. You now are free to do this because you have properly framed the problem and attained alignment at each step along the way. Although *Solution Design* is not quite a victory lap, it allows you the creative flexibility to demonstrate that not only can you set goals, but you can also conjure up innovative ways to deliver value to the users.

You have substantial leeway, with respect to the possible directions you can take, because this step hinges on the pain points that you identified in the previous steps (and the personas or cohorts for whom you will solve them). Some practical tips for approaching this step include:

- Provide several different options for solutions that solve the desired problem. You can further prioritize these options, time and circumstances permitting. You should justify your recommended solution based on its anticipated impact.

- Outline the different parts of the solution that will need to be built in order to demonstrate your understanding of the various moving pieces. Does your solution require a UI, such as an admin tool? To back up your suggestions, you can reference some examples from other products, such as competitors, or even your own past experience.

- What metrics would you want to track to determine the success of the improvement or features? Why did you pick those?

- Is what you selected the minimum viable (least complex) version? You may want to articulate *more* functionality that would be required for the first version, and then actively reduce your development scope to an MVP before your conclusion.

- Do you have ideas for the rollout plan? You may want to highlight some ways that you could experiment (A/B test) in order to optimize your launch or discuss whether you might want to release the feature, at least initially, only to a subset of users.

In execution case questions, the Solution Design step is a bit different. You are not necessarily suggesting a feature, but rather an action plan of what you'd do next. Given the scenario presented— such as a drop in a core metric—you would summarize what product metrics you'd analyze, segmented by the appropriate cohort of users, and what actionable steps you would take if you had all the information that you needed.

Because you are working your way through the framework, you do not have to design or think up solution designs on the spot. You have ample time to dissect various products (especially the company's products) and brainstorm improvements in advance of the interview as part of your preparation. The framework allows you to demonstrate your structured thinking and competence while pursuing a logical conclusion. If you do end up discussing a product with which you are not familiar, proceed slowly and deliberately and think about adding features that worked in other apps you've used in your daily life.

Lastly, here's a look at our example, continued from Step 4:

Step 1: Outline a Vision and Identify the North Star Metric	
Company	Music-streaming service
Vision	The world is better with more music in it.
North Star Metric	Songs streamed
Step 2: Highlight Strategic Themes	
Strategic Themes	• Provide all music available for free on the streaming platform (Competitive Developments)

	• Keep listeners engaged with personalized recommendations (Business Goals) • Allow for easy sharing and social playlists (Business Goals)
Steps 3 & 4: Explore Relevant Personas or Cohorts and and User Journey and Pain Points	
Personas or Cohorts	• Exerciser - Pain Point: Don't want to have to manipulate their music many times during a session - Impact: More songs streamed, higher weekly retention • Office Worker - Pain Point: Recommendations must not be too distracting from work - Impact: Longer sessions, more songs streamed • Host (entertainer) - Pain Point: Continuous music in the same vibe or genre - Impact: Higher weekly retention
Step 5: Provide a Solution Design	
Solution Design (Proposed Solution)	We should build a feature called "My Routines" that creates a weekday work playlist on Monday based on the music the user listens to from 9 to 5, Monday through Friday, and another playlist on Saturday morning based on the music the user listens to while he is running. We can use the GPS location to determine when the user is running vs. when he is in the office. This solves the pain points for the Exerciser and the Office Worker personas and will result in longer session times and more songs streamed per user, per week.

Note: Cross-functional relationships

You can score some extra credit by touching on cross-functional partners that you'd want to leverage in order to accomplish your hypothetical goal. As we have touted throughout *Product Sense*, the relationships you build with the other functional areas and teams are tantamount to both your success as a PM and the success of your product. Mentioning how you would leverage and empower the work of your colleagues and peers, in order to release successful features, is a great value add.

> *Example: "What we would do to bring this feature to market is first validate it with our sales and ops teams, and then slowly ramp the feature up to our customers on a rolling basis to ensure we are hitting observable movements in metrics X, Y, and Z."*

You are stating what we should build, and why. The most important PM question!

Another walk-through: Execution

In the last section, we walked through the steps of the Compass Framework and applied them to an improvement for a hypothetical music-streaming service, with the goal of increasing weekly retention. We demonstrated how the framework can be used to help you think through any product or feature. You should repeat the exercise in the context of many different companies, especially those with which you will interview. The practice time you invest in this exercise will also help you think like a product manager on the team you are seeking to join. In addition, it will help you come into an interview well prepared to discuss strategy as if you had already thought through the case questions you are presented with.

Let's consider how this framework applies to execution questions. Remember, execution questions relate to how you think about a product in terms of KPIs and data. Such questions usually come as potential scenarios such as a certain key metric changing unexpectedly or evaluation of a trade-off. For simplicity's sake, we'll stick to our previously used example of a music-streaming service as our product of choice.

Scenario: Weekly active users have dropped 10%

Step 1: Outline a Vision and Identify the North Star Metric	
Company	Music-streaming service
Vision	The world is better with more music in it.
North Star Metric	Songs streamed
Step 2: Highlight Strategic Themes	
Strategic Themes	• Provide all music available for free on the streaming platform (Competitive Developments) • Keep listeners engaged with personalized recommendations (Business Goals) • • Allow for easy sharing and social playlists (Business Goals)

The product's vision and strategy shouldn't vary with the type of question and, even in the scenario above, we still need to evaluate the problem and appropriately contextualize the space in which the company is operating (as a framing device for which cohorts or users the PM should investigate, as well as any solutions).

Step 3: Explore Relevant Personas or Cohorts	

Personas or Cohorts	• Geographic Cohorts: Is only North America, the EU, or APAC affected or are users across all geographies declining?
	• Sign-up Date Cohorts:
	  a. Are the users who most recently signed up dropping off?
	  b. How is the retention rate of users that joined a long time ago?
	• Engagement Cohorts:

| | a. | Are users who have typically used the product every day beginning to lapse? |
| | b. | Are occasional users failing to return to the product within expected windows? |

Notice how we chose cohorts here (recall the differences between cohorts and personas in Chapter 3). Why? Because, in this case, we are analyzing data, as indicated by the interviewer's question relating to a decline in weekly active users. We are first asking key metric questions, in order to effectively isolate this decline in users via some shared characteristic that will help us resolve the issue.

Step 4: User Journey	
Shared metrics	• # new accounts created • # of songs played on a weekly basis • # playlists created • Unique artists/user • # Ads shown • Session length

For this step, instead of exploring a full user journey as we might do in a product design question (for which our goal is to identify pain points), we are analyzing key metrics that represent user behavior within the streaming app. Essentially, this is a brainstorm of things that might help point us in the right direction toward understanding why our app is rapidly losing users each week. The next step is to analyze this with respect to the cohorts we identified in the previous step and articulate a narrative of where the problem might lie.

During this and also the previous step, your interviewer may give you clues about whether certain metrics are causing the issue; they may explicitly state if a certain metric has gone up or down, which will help you hone in on the right answer.

In this example, let's assume that you've learned from your discussion with the interviewer that the decline in weekly average users can be isolated to new users who are retaining at a lower rate than the historical average. There does not appear to be a technical explanation for the decline, so we suspect that there may be some kind of external factors at play or unmet expectations with respect to the user experience in the product today.

Step 5: Provide a Solution Design	
Solution Design (Proposed Solution)	You might discuss with your interviewer the behaviors common to new app users. (In this case, setting up an initial playlist, searching for songs/artists, or discovering new music.) Is a certain feature particularly predictive of higher engagement and retention? If so, propose a way to more aggressively surface an appropriate feature or decrease the friction obstructing the user in their initial encounter with the difficult feature.

As you can see, the Compass Framework steps can be applied to all question types you might face in the interview process, specifically case questions. Be sure to practice them thoroughly in advance of your interviews to ensure that you'll be more confident and conversational during those conversations.

Change course based on your interviewer's feedback

One of the key things that can (and almost certainly will) happen during the course of a case interview is that the interviewer will change the context or add additional details. She will also potentially steer you in a different direction if she feels that you are headed down the wrong path or are stuck. That is OK! What matters in this situation is how you react to feedback and changes on the fly. Your interviewer will be trying to gauge culture fit as well as hard PM skills; so, if you are receptive to different ideas and are collaborative during the interview process, your calm and constructive reaction will earn you additional points with your interviewer.

It is also a good idea to engage your interviewer as much as possible each step of the way by asking what she thinks—try to not go too deep into an area or progress too far without getting a sense of whether the interviewer is aligned with your direction. You might say something like:

- "I am going to first step back and think about the goals here. What do you think?"

- "I am thinking of prioritizing these ideas . . . how do you feel about these criteria?"

- "Something you were saying earlier resonated with me . . . could you tell me more about that?"

As much as possible, connecting with the interviewer as a peer and solving the case together will make you appear more confident and professional, like an amiable future colleague! The more you practice, the more you will feel confident doing this.

Summarizing the Compass Framework

For those who are facing the prospect of doing PM interviews for the first time, it can feel a bit like preparing for the SATs or MCATs. However, a more productive mindset might be to view the interviews as your chance to demonstrate your understanding of all of the concepts of the WSB problem. It might feel uncomfortably rigid to try to fit every type of product case question into a framework, but as you repeat the process and continually practice the framework it will begin to feel more natural. It's also key to remember that, in actuality, the concepts you must demonstrate in the interview are no different from the fundamentals you will employ when you are a PM on a team. You are simply performing the job that you are seeking in a hypothetical context in order to demonstrate to your interviewer that you are the right candidate to hire.

The five steps of the Compass Framework are designed to guide you through an excellent showing for your interviewer, while hitting on the key rubric categories you need along the way.

It's not rocket science, but in order to make a career change in product management, you need to adopt the mindset of a PM, know what a good process looks like, and have a solid framework for solving the WSB problem. Then, you need to show that process off in an interview. Following the Compass Framework is a simple, yet effective, way to showcase your skills and pave the way to getting hired by a top company.

CHAPTER 9

Putting it into Action

As we know, the Compass Framework breaks the WSB concepts into five steps. Here is a visualization of this process.

As each individual question you might be asked is unique, there is no silver-bullet solution that will help you answer every question you might encounter within an interview. However, the key is to demonstrate your command of the fundamentals. Any PM candidate can rattle off buzzwords gleaned from reading the tech blogs, but only a practiced one can illustrate concepts live, in an unfamiliar setting, with a stranger sitting across from them. The five steps listed above won't save you if you are not well prepared, but they are your ticket to crafting a well-rounded plan for a dynamic interview that will impress your prospective company.

To illustrate the framework further, let's look at six sample responses and the case-question types each focuses on.

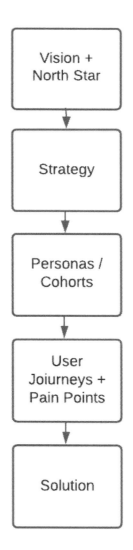

Sample Responses to Case Questions

Let's get our hands dirty with some example questions, and practice utilizing the Compass Framework in order to answer them.

In the following section, we will provide a product case question followed by some commentary about how to structure your answer. Then, we will provide a possible response with guidance on how we would approach solving the case. In each example, we've inserted the framework steps **(in parentheses and bold type)** to show you how each part of the response maps to them.

To get the maximum benefit, we recommend trying to answer these questions on your own before viewing our answers, which will give you an unbiased look at your understanding of the framework. While off the cuff—real-life responses might not be as eloquent as these written examples—you will at least get a sense of the framework in action and experience thinking through various case scenarios.

1. What is your favorite product and why?

Profile Company: Spotify

Question Type: Product Sense and Design

Tell me about a product you like. What do you like about it? How would you improve it?

Commentary: This is one of the most commonly used questions in PM interviews, and you will very likely be presented with it at some point. The good news is that it's an easy one to prepare for. While you don't want to sound too rehearsed, you can prepare for this question by thinking about products you know well and how to dissect them (you might want to refer back to the product audit we outlined in Chapter 3). Generally speaking, avoid hardware products such as the iPhone or a Tesla. Complex products such as those could cause the interviewer to bring you down a path you haven't prepared for, while products with a smaller scope will help you maintain control of the interview's flow. Consider focusing on products that have a smaller set of use cases; for example, a to-do-list app, a ride-sharing app, or a music-discovery platform. You can practice at home using a few different products that you know, looking at the features that help make them successful (or not!). That way, you will have several options to deploy, depending on the type of company you will be interviewing with, or in the event that the interviewer asks you to pick a certain type of product.

For this example, we will examine Spotify. This is a product that is widely known, has evolved its strategy over time, and has invested in substantial feature development and general improvements. Additionally, there are several major competitors in the music-streaming market, so a discussion around competitive strategy will be relevant.

Response:

I use Spotify almost every day. Outside of being a regular user, I am also excited about the problems they are solving with respect to connecting their members and users to new and interesting music (**Vision**). Because they operate in a relatively crowded space, where the access to a large catalog of music is ubiquitous, they have doubled down in two areas: discovery through social connections (**Strategic Theme**) and machine learning powering personalized playlists (**Strategic Theme**) to move the needle on discovery. I would suspect that a key metric to measure progress toward the discovery goal is the number of unique artists discovered, per user (**North Star Metric**).

What I like about Spotify is that it solves an important pain point for me. My use case for a music-streaming service is primarily during working hours for at least several hours each day (**Persona**). I don't want to have to actively monitor and select music each time a song ends (**Pain Point**); I need a regular stream of new music catered to my taste that helps me do focused work.

The "Discover Weekly" feature has been beneficial for my work productivity because, based on my previous listening history, I'm served a fresh playlist of new songs every week. Spotify automatically identifies and adapts as I continue to listen to music. If I were the PM for Discover Weekly, I would add the ability to share my weekly playlist with colleagues, or vice versa (**Pain Point**). If, for example, someone I know has good taste in music, it would be nice to follow their tastes over time or even listen concurrently with them (**Solution**). As a user, I would discover new artists that I might not have already known, which would likely benefit Spotify's North Star metrics—user retention and paid subscribers.

2. How would you improve a product?

Profile Company: Facebook Groups
Question Type: Product Execution

> *You are the PM leading Facebook Groups and you notice that the number of users creating new groups has decreased, month*

*over month. What is your plan to investigate and counteract
this trend?*

Commentary: This is a prototypical product execution case question.
It requires you to dissect an existing product into its key metrics, and
determine an investigation and improvement plan.

Response:

As the PM on Facebook Groups and faced with this drop in feature
engagement, I would first dig into understanding whether this is a
problem. My plan would be to (1) understand the user segments
important to the health of this feature, (2) evaluate the key feature
metrics and demonstrate what they mean for the business, (3)
prioritize these metrics, and (4) state the direction I think the team
should take given the information that we have.

We should first understand why we should care about improving
this metric. The goal of Facebook Groups is to deepen engagement
for Facebook users by creating spaces for users to discuss topics with
like-minded individuals **(Vision).** The product value for the
business would be: Facebook expects that users who are also Group
members will visit Facebook more frequently **(Strategic Theme)**,
either increasing time spent or sessions per week, and engaging in
Newsfeed content **(Strategic Theme)**, since the posts from their
Groups will surface there, further increasing time spent on
Facebook. Facebook wants time on site to be meaningful to the user,
and time spent engaging with other users might be an important key
metric **(North Star Metric)**. The drop we have observed in Groups
may coincide with a drop in other engagement metrics. However,
we could argue that fewer Groups being created might mean that

users are feeling adequately served or better served by the existing Groups, so we should further discuss that possibility later.

Given the understanding above, I'd evaluate funnel metrics within the context of various user segments. I'd explore whether this drop is localized to one specific segment of users (**Personas**). I'd want to know if this decline in the creation of Groups is specific to a certain geographic area. I would also analyze whether the decline is specific to a certain Facebook Group category; for example, is it skewed toward political groups, which might be explained by current events or an election cycle.

Next, I would try to understand how the metrics related to the feature are impacting our important business metrics (**User Journey**). I would segment my metrics into three buckets: Acquisition, Activation, and Conversion.

At the top of the funnel, I would evaluate whether there is an overall drop in usage of Groups, since such a drop could similarly affect Group creation. Then I would assess whether the success rate for the sequence of steps (funnel) required to create a Group has changed and consider whether some part of the sequence might need refinement. Lastly, I would need to understand the compositions by type of users creating Groups: are they users creating Groups for the first time or are they seasoned community builders? The drop in total Groups could be explained further if we knew that the average Groups created per unique creator was down, or if there was a decline in unique users creating Groups.

To further understand this lagging indicator, our team would then investigate the types of Groups that are being created and analyze behaviors within these Groups. A hypothesis could be that certain recently created Groups are serving an underserved niche and that a decline in Groups being created may be expected over time as the feature reaches maturity and the accumulated user need "debt" is met and drawn down. I'd also want to evaluate the mix of private and public Groups, to determine a bit more the characteristics of the Groups that are actually declining. I would also want to note, of the Groups that are being created, what percent of them are we seeing grow to a reasonable member size—because if the trend for "active" Groups isn't declining (or is increasing), then it might not be a metric to worry about.

A summary of this analysis could be visualized in a table, which I'll draw for you on the whiteboard:

Top of the Funnel	Activation	Retention
Is the drop related to fewer users creating Groups?	Are there issues with the types of Groups being created or the creation process?	How successful are the Groups?
<ul><li>Groups/creators</li><li>Groups by geography</li><li>Groups created by device type</li></ul>	<ul><li>Groups created, by category</li><li># Groups per users (Group fatigue)</li><li>Completion rate of Group-creation steps</li></ul>	<ul><li>Average Group growth size overall</li><li>Activity of Groups</li><li>Growth rates of different Group categories</li></ul>

Finally, to put it all together, I would formulate a plan of action for our team (**Solution**). If the decline in Group creation is a broken or leaky funnel, we could flesh out a roadmap geared toward optimizing the existing flows.

If we're facing Group feature fatigue, excessive numbers of certain Group types, or some other fundamental user problem, we'd want to create a feature or optimization to tackle the larger problem. Creating new Group category types, incentivizing and suggesting early adoption of Groups, or some other new feature, could be our next step. Once we evaluate the required metrics, we'd take the appropriate next action.

3. How would you build a product to pursue a new strategic goal?

Profile Company: Twitter for E-commerce
Question Type: Product Sense and Design (or Product Strategy)

How would you design Twitter for e-commerce?

Commentary: This is a tricky question because it could potentially be interpreted as *two* different case categories: Product Strategy and Product Sense and Design. The word "design" might, at first glance, suggest that you should index heavily on the user journeys and solutions of the product and quickly narrow in on a single feature. However, the strategic framing is a hidden gambit of this challenge; why *would* Twitter consider an e-commerce vertical and how should it position its business model? It might be a good idea to challenge the implicit assumption made in this question. So, in our response, you may notice that we focus more on the "why" and the "who" to better cover our strategic themes. If the interviewer points you in another direction, you may need to adapt and go with the flow. Explore different directions for your answers during your own practice to see what you feel most comfortable with.

Response:

Twitter has become an integral part of society, culture, and politics—and has a myriad of strategic directions in which it could proceed in the future. The leadership team must be asking what strategies will continue to bolster the company's key metrics and, ultimately, fund business expansion with new verticals.

Before suggesting any product development direction, let's take a step back to examine why Twitter would consider an e-commerce approach as part of its product-strategy playbook.

Twitter is, and continually aspires to be, the world's leading real-time content and discussion platform (**Vision**). Executing on this vision requires Twitter to (**1**) invest in the growth of its loyal users, (**2**) establish strong publisher relationships through content creator tools, and (**3**) disseminate the information to the right eyes using personalized recommendations (**Strategic Themes**).

Its success as a platform should be measured by user engagement, a proxy for users' trust in information shown on Twitter, and that information's relevancy compared to other news sources (**North Star Metric**). Based on a potential need for an incremental revenue stream, in addition to advertising, we'd approach monetization through the lens of publisher relationships and tools supporting creation of new and enticing content. Our metric of success, again, would be user engagement, which would be improved through acquiring and retaining prominent and successful content creators. Thus, providing these creators with tools to monetize their content would create an invaluable platform—for users to get content that they can't get anywhere else—and further establish Twitter as the dominant player in real-time-news content.

E-commerce on Twitter, as a strategy, would relate to the publisher- and creator-tools arm of the strategy playbook. By continuing to support content publishers with tools to not only create content but also build a business on the platform, Twitter would benefit from higher-engaged publishers who would create more content to distribute to the rest of Twitter's users. Twitter could also explore a new monetization vertical through this initiative. However, I would stress that the first goal in this "zero-to-one" initiative should be to increase the engagement of content creators, media, and brands, and for net revenue to become a goal in subsequent milestones.

To determine the best feature and product roadmap that would drive e-commerce revenue, we would want to evaluate what we are trying to solve, and for whom, prior to suggesting the design. Our stated plan for success is that we want to help brand and media organizations monetize better and thus engage deeper on the platform. With this as our goal, it would be important to evaluate several of the types of users along this direction (**Personas).**

Persona evaluation

Persona	Needs	Pain Points	Impact
Consumers	Find relevant products based on interests	Purchase destinations separated from where they consume news content	Higher conversion if friction is reduced
Small Business Owners	Build brand, Sell product	Must create ecommerce site themselves	Reduced costs to run business and increased sales
Enterprises	Build brand, communicate with customers and understand their needs	Hard to establish dialogue with users	Higher enterprise engagement on platform
Influencers	Satisfy business customers, build brand, create compelling content	Insufficient content-creation tools to achieve their goals, audience size	More content created on platform, increased engagement

We see the highest upside—in terms of reach and growth toward our North Star—in the influencers market. Unfortunately for Twitter, influencers are stepping outside of the platform to create partnerships with brands or to sell merchandise based on their style and personality, which represents an opportunity to monetize their personal brand. If we can reduce the friction for influencers to monetize, we can coax them into moving their influencer businesses onto Twitter.

Journey Step	Pain Point	Potential Opportunity	Impact
Selling branded merchandise	• Have to design themselves • Need to find suppliers	Create tools that allow users to create merchandise utilizing existing, Twitter-approved suppliers	Revenue and Engagement
Identifying potential brand partnerships	• Influencers are represented by agency taking cut	Twitter builds a marketplace to bring brands to influencers	Revenue
Gathering affiliate revenue	• Can promote products for a commission, must go outside	Twitter can allow infeed purchasing of products. Can provide a marketplace of affiliate goods	Revenue

Based on the table above, the most compelling candidate with the largest potential impact might be the brand-partnership marketplace. There are already direct connections to advertisers who may be interested in an additional channel and Twitter occupies a unique position to be able to democratize these deals to the masses (allowing even micro-influencers to promote brands).

4. Evaluating a Trade-off

Profile Company: YouTube
Question Type: Product Execution

You are a PM on YouTube and you have tested a feature that increases the number of video starts by five percent (good) but also increases video-load time by five percent (bad). Do you release the feature?

Commentary: This is a variant on a Product Execution question that seeks to determine how you would analyze a product and articulate the important data points needed in order to make a confident decision about a feature or change to that product. For this question you will still dig deeply into the product metrics but, instead of diagnosing a problem, you will consider two parts of an equation in order to state which of two alternatives is superior (i.e., the trade-off). Product managers evaluate trade-offs all the time; it makes sense that many FAANG companies ask about trade-offs in their interviews.

When faced with a trade-off question, ask yourself:

- Is the trade-off especially clear? In this example question it is, but in other instances it may be more ambiguous.

- Think about potential ripple effects for each side of the trade-off. If load time increases by five percent what happens to the user? What else could this mean?

- Can you find that common currency that balances both sides using a North Star Metric or Vision?

Response:

Consumers are increasingly gravitating toward short video content online to consume news, entertainment, how-to videos, and more. This has been accelerating in recent years and, although there are many products and services driving this trend, YouTube is one of the most dominant.

YouTube is democratizing video-content creation and distributing it to every human on earth for free (**Vision**). To achieve this, over the years they've introduced robust creation tools to edit and produce high-quality content, strong personalized-recommendation tools, and strong advertising technology to scale the growth of the platform (**Strategic Themes**). Ongoing feature development would further increase the quality and number of creators, measurable by the growth of successful, contributing video creators (**North Star Metric**).

This new feature potentially represents both good and bad news. Video starts have increased, which could indicate that more users are watching videos. However, load times have also increased, which could mean a degraded user experience (since users presumably do not enjoy waiting to watch their videos). Are longer load times being experienced by every user? We should confirm whether this is the case. Let's map this out on the whiteboard (**User Journey**).

User Group	Importance / Hypothesis
Device Type	Assess whether longer load times are localized to older machines, browsers, or devices.
Video Type	Are longer-form videos taking longer to load or is the issue persistent across all videos? Alternatively, are more starts coming from a specific category or categories of videos?
YouTube Subscribers	To what degree are our YouTube Red subscribers adversely affected by longer load times?

The table I've drawn for you represents some cohorts we should consider during our trade-off analysis. We should also analyze the rest of the funnel to determine what is important (and at stake) here (**Solution Design**). Let me illustrate this:

KPI	Load Time	Starts Increase	Comments
Revenue	• # of pre-roll ads shown • Total number of ads shown	• Total number of ads shown to users • Engagement in ads (CTR) • Total revenue per users	We want to identify whether the number of ads shown decreases based on a higher number of users leaving before the video loads.
Engagement	• Bounce rate • Subscriber growth per channel • Comments/likes	• Total number of videos watched per user per day • Total time spent on YouTube • Retention of users • Shares (to others)	From an engagement perspective, we are assessing whether the number of users who drop off due to the increased loading time adversely affects retention or overall time spent in the app.

Based on the plan I've drawn for you, the decision to release the feature depends on whether or not the number of users who bounce off the page (leave without viewing content) has an effect on the monetization of or engagement with YouTube. Since our North Star is the number of creators, we should closely monitor if the number of users who bounce is affecting either engagement in terms of subscribing to channels or monetization (via ad views), since monetization is a key driver for creators to post new content.

5. Measuring Success

Profile Company: Reddit Ads
Question Type: Product Execution

> *You've just become the PM at Reddit, focusing on the ad platform. How would you define success?*

Commentary: Some interview questions may require you to figure out what success looks like. The good news is that these KPI and metrics questions fit in well with the Product Execution examples that we have been using thus far. Analyze the important metrics—with slight variations depending on the context of the question—so that the same principles apply, but understand that the flow of the response will be different. As we have discussed, be sure to carefully frame the problem at the beginning! Defining success for a feature or product area will depend on where the company is compared to its strategy, competitors, and overall vision.

Response:

Great question! Let's first frame the problem because we shouldn't measure the success of the ads product without first understanding Reddit's overall strategic position as a company.

Reddit occupies a space that is part community and part media consumption. Its objective is to be the world's most engaging forum for discussing current events and personal interests **(Vision)**. There is a community for everyone at Reddit and the company can track engaged users as a means of measuring the progress toward that lofty goal **(North Star Metric)**. We see Reddit investing in community-development features for moderators, trust-and-safety tools to keep the ecosystem safe, and relevant and personalized news feeds for users (**Strategic Themes**). Given these themes, the ads product ought to fit into the business such that it doesn't distract from the growth of new communities or the retention of users based on their newsfeed engagement.

The success of the ads product needs to be considered from three angles—the advertiser, the user, and Reddit (**Personas**).

Persona	Wants/Needs/ Motivations	Current Pain Points	What Success Looks Like for this Persona	Success Metric
Advertiser	Buyers are already interested in the subject matter	Some obscure topics or interests are hard to reach on existing platforms	Wants a low price per user and high conversion rate	ROI
Reddit User	Different types of users have different tolerances for ads	Irrelevant ads can cause poor experiences	Enjoy Reddit content with less frequent, but more useful, ads	Engagement and retention
Reddit	A large amount of advertisers to increase demand	Likely difficult to balance targeted ads in a semi-anonymous forum	Value for customer while maintaining a healthy net margin	CPM (effective cost per thousand ad impressions)

Given these goals, and coming from a three-pronged approach, I would recommend analyzing these KPIs from each of these angles.

Advertiser	User	Reddit
• Cost per Action • Reach • ROI	• Retention by number of ads shown • Ad click-through rate	• Number of advertisers bidding • Revenue per 1000 ads

Since our initial goal was for Reddit to deliver relevant ads that don't annoy its users, our success could be measured by Advertiser return on investment (ROI). Since advertisers see returns when users engage with their products after seeing an ad, this metric has both a supply and demand component. We should measure long-term retention as a counter metric, since advertisers see returns in the shorter and medium term.

6. Evaluating a Trade-off

Profile Company: Netflix
Question Type: Product Execution

> *You're the PM tasked with optimizing Netflix's home screen. How do you determine how shows get promoted? Should they be promoted editorially, or recommended algorithmically?*

Commentary: This question asks you to assess a trade-off—whether the curated selection (i.e., original content) is better than programmatically personalized results. You'll need to think both strategically, as well as think analytically when examining the trade-off.

We should assume that the curated content is most likely determined by a team that picks the latest original content or newest premier catalog additions. On the other hand, we should assume that the algorithmic selection that this question mentions implies personalized solutions tailored to the users' likes and dislikes. However, it might be useful to dive deep into what that means in the answer, as well. One might be tempted to mention Netflix's original goal to democratize all content and allow users to "cut the cord," abandoning cable providers. However, that might not resonate as strongly with an interviewer at Netflix of today, as the platform has gone through substantial changes in user behaviors and is now part of a very competitive landscape. Nowadays, the competition is stiff and there is a constant fight for content and engaged users.

Response:

Netflix strives to provide the world with on-demand, high-quality, and original entertainment content (**Vision**). Success for Netflix means that their users choose Netflix over alternatives such as cable and other streaming providers, as measured by user retention (**North Star Metric**), month over month.

While Netflix was first to market in the streaming space, its first-mover advantage has waned over the last few years as stiff competition has emerged from content owners via heavy platform investment (think Hulu and Disney Plus). Consequently, Netflix has reduced its dependence on licensed movies and series. Their current strategic initiatives in this space are: original programming, personalized recommendations, and technology (**Strategy**). Netflix retains users by pairing the highest-quality streaming experience with the best user experience through a combination of the three aforementioned initiatives.

Strategically, Netflix needs to find a balance between offering original content versus personalizing recommendations. To do so, we would need to fully understand the user types that factor into our analysis, since user segments might react differently. Let's segment by engagement buckets: low, medium, and high (**Personas**).

Engagement Bucket	Motivation	Churn Risk (Likely to Leave)	Favorite Content
Low	These users visit Netflix infrequently, perhaps several times each month and likely use other streaming providers but keep Netflix since it has some shows they can't get elsewhere.	High	Original Content
Medium	These users will watch a few shows consistently, or the occasional movie on weekends.	High	Partner Programming
High	These are daily Netflix users, likely viewing on multiple devices and constantly looking for new shows or movies to watch, as well as re-watching old favorites.	Low	Partner Programming

Remember that Netflix wants to deliver the best experience to its viewers—with an eye toward maintaining high retention and engagement—by investing in original content, recommendations, and technology. Let's evaluate development through the lens of engagement buckets.

We need to understand what the trade-off is between editorial and personalized recommendations. In a space where one show is promoted, other shows will not be. Netflix has to strategically position its app so that it gains and retains the most eyes on the platform relative to other streaming platforms.

So, what do we need to think about to determine if the editorial content is successful?

- **Stickiness**: When a user interacts with original content, how likely is it that the user comes back again the following week?

- **Completion**: How likely is it that a given piece of selected content is completed?

- **Viral Tendencies**: Does a particular show generate word-of-mouth growth?

- **Press**: Is there an upcoming award show or other outside event that would draw eyeballs to Netflix apps?

What do we need to measure to know if the programmatic content is successful? For example:

- **Series Progress:** Will the user finish watching a series soon?

- **Genre Similar**: Does this user have unwatched content, while other types of users have a higher completion rate?

- **Netflix Catalog**: How much of the total catalog, by genre, is currently being watched by users? Would adding content to some of the underutilized genres create more demand for Netflix?

The original question asked us to determine what the framework should be for deciding the "above-the-fold" content section on Netflix. What we have determined is the structure of deciding how to balance this:

- When curated content is suggested, it might promote growth for a piece of content, a genre, or for Netflix overall.

- A programmatic piece of content would be personalized to users' preferences, trying to keep a current user engaged with content that, going forward, keeps that user retained.

Let's return to our user-segment table. With consideration for our North Star Metric (user churn), we should evaluate based on our likely-to-churn cohorts, which are low- or medium-engaged users. We want to improve retention and churn at Netflix, given our strategy and vision.

Our strategy would amount to showing original and curated content to low- and medium-engaged users more frequently, based on the knowledge that they may be using Netflix nonexclusively (**User Journey**).

We'd want to measure this hypothesis by assessing the following:

- If low-engaged users watch a new and original show, are they more likely to increase their **number of Netflix sessions** in a week?

- If users do not watch an original show, are they **more likely to churn** than users who do?

- How does the click-through rate change for users who view no curated content versus. those who view a substantial amount of curated content?

In the case where editorial content significantly decreases retention for users in the "highly engaged" bucket, we'd likely want to pursue a strategy of all personalized recommendations.

For analysis of the trade-off, we'd need to work with our PR, Content, and Product Marketing teams to determine the timing and priority of editorial content **(Solution Design)**. When a piece of content is trending, we may fuel more platform growth by promoting that content more aggressively on the Netflix home screen. Additionally, award-show nominations (and when the award show is aired) may periodically skew selection—because a nomination or an award will give Netflix more credibility, which may lead to more signups.

CHAPTER 10

Additional Case-Question Tips

If you use the structure provided by the Compass Framework, and adhere to aligning on goals first, you will already be ahead of the game. Yet, it's important to not only know the framework inside and out, but also to relay information confidently. A strong response to answering questions includes not only the individual pieces of the framework, but also confidence in presenting them and ability to be flexible if the interviewer pushes you in different directions. In this section, we'll include some tips on how to achieve that confidence which sets great candidates apart from the pool.

Structured Thinking

Demonstrating your structured thinking and communication abilities to your interviewer will show her that you can approach and deconstruct a problem in a logical way and make it easier to manage and solve. In a PM interview, that also means simplifying the problem with guide rails and constraints and applying a set of criteria to weigh competing solutions. Using the Compass Framework in each answer you formulate will convey that you are a good decision maker who can confidently explain why one idea has more value than another.

PMs don't need to have the *best* ideas but they must help the team focus on the *right* ones.

To illustrate this more saliently, here are some examples of structured thinking from everyday life:

- Making a decision using a pros/cons list

- Determining the best return on an investment (over multiple options)

- Writing out a to-do list with multiple workstreams (e.g.,, work, childcare, home improvement)

- Planning your exercise schedule for the week

- Developing and managing a personal or family budget

In an interview situation, it is of utmost importance that you demonstrate a method to your madness. The Compass Framework will help to keep you on point. You can go off on a little tangent here and there, as long as you maintain your focus and continue to follow the framework steps. As for presenting your thinking in a structured manner, here are some tips:

- **For a remote interview, keep notes or post-its on your desk, out of sight.** Your research on the company, product, the Compass Framework, or other structured-communication tools that you might want to remind yourself to use during an interview can be great resources to have in front of you when interviewing remotely. We all become nervous and forget things in high-pressure situations. Hedge your dependency on your flawed human memory by plastering your workstation with quick references to which you can refer, in a pinch.

- **Utilize a white board.** Nothing helps to organize your argument more than to demonstrate it visually. During most PM interviews, you will have a whiteboard available to you. In the event that you don't, be sure to bring pen and paper. If the interview is being conducted over video call, ask the interviewer if it's possible to use the whiteboard feature or screen share your own desktop. You may even want to invest in a handheld whiteboard for an interview that you take from your home.

- **Clarify first.** Don't jump straight into answering the question. Take a second, pause, and work with your interviewer to confirm your understanding of what is being asked. When you reach the point of applying structure, you will need to have a desired outcome to which everyone is aligned. Without this, you will run the risk of not answering the question according to expectations and will need to course correct during your answer, which could cost you some momentum.

Applying structure is what sets good candidates apart from the rest of the pack. Don't begin proposing solutions without first framing the problem.

Process Over Problem Solving

The interviewers may not care exactly what solution you come up with. The PM interview is primarily about demonstrating that you have a sound *process* for arriving at a solution.

Every company is full of smart people that have great ideas. They will not hire you for your great ideas (as sad as that might sound!). They will hire you because you can help the rest of the organization arrive at the smartest, most impactful, business-critical solutions. They will also hire you to ensure that the solutions on which you're trying to reach alignment are built (and operated) as optimally as possible. The more that you can demonstrate a sound problem-solving process, the better off you will be. Following the Compass Framework will help you highlight these talents and skills.

Be Collaborative

If you can demonstrate that you'd be the type of PM that is easy to work with, someone who can strategize and brainstorm well with others, and an overall collaborative person, you will stand out. Confidence comes from working with your interviewers, not against them.

Be sure to ask questions, probe them for their thoughts, and be flexible based on any feedback they may throw your way. When interviewing with employees in different disciplines—engineering, marketing, or design, for example—it's even more crucial to manage perception of your soft skills. These types of people are most likely interviewing you because you will partner directly with them. They are looking for your culture fit and to see if they can imagine getting along with you from day to day. If they will be spending a significant amount of time with you, they certainly want to be sure that you will be compatible with them. A workplace is a medium for product development but also for camaraderie, solving challenges together, and enjoying the ride. Be humble, be excited, and be collaborative.

You Can Do This

Thus far, we hope we have demonstrated that product management is a balanced blend of good design, strong analytics, user empathy, and persistent execution. The resulting product is best when a PM can orchestrate all of these areas seamlessly. To design an impactful feature, analyze its progress, react to changes, and communicate plans effectively is what makes product management a multidisciplinary art.

We have tried to convey—throughout this first section of the book, and especially through the sample responses to case questions—that the Compass Framework can be an effective tool for answering interview questions, and is paramount to solving the WSB problem. We did not just regurgitate some buzzwords and rigidly apply a framework; on the contrary, our aim was to show you how to confidently articulate your own strengths as the unique PM you are (and will be), in a structured way that your interviewer will clearly see.

To be best prepared, you will need to practice using the framework and applying the concepts we have covered. Mock interviews are an excellent way to get the feel for a real interview encounter. Find a partner who is on the same interview path and work together. Practice every aspect of the interview experience: from answering case questions, to illustrating your thoughts on a whiteboard or a piece of notebook paper, to entering and exiting the room. Leave no stone unturned! Find lists of PM questions online and go through them. Once you have landed an interview, focus your preparations and practice on that company's products and strengths. Understand their core KPIs and where they sit competitively against the rest of the industry. Practice makes perfect.

The next part of the book focuses on the process PMs go through when they are actively looking for a job. When you feel prepared enough to do so, and confident in your ability to answer the WSB problem, these final steps will guide you through getting your next job in Product.

CHAPTER 11

Behavioral and Culture Questions

We have focused our content so far on case questions and how to answer them because these are the most rigorous and require the most preparation. However, structure permitting, many interviewers also engage candidates in small talk or ask other questions to assess a candidate's skill set or culture fit for the team or company.

Behavioral questions will require you to speak to current or past professional experiences and how you may have reacted to certain situations. These often assume the form of "tell me about a time you . . ." You should be prepared to calmly and concisely answer questions like the following:

- Tell me about a time you had a serious disagreement with a colleague and how you resolved it.

- Tell me about a time you failed and what you learned from the experience. How would you approach the same situation now, if given the chance?

- What's your greatest professional weakness and how do you overcome it? Can you give me an example using a project you worked on?

To give you our perspective on how to approach behavioral questions, here are our top tips:

1. Look into "STAR," a framework that is commonly used by PMs and consultants to answer behavioral questions.

"STAR" is an acronym that stands for **S**ituation, **T**ask, **A**ctions, **R**esults. Hit key points in each of those four steps, and you will have a coherent and complete answer.

2. Think back on your work experience thus far and identify any major initiatives you've worked on that you can speak to within just a few minutes. Write out scripts for these initiatives based on the STAR framework. Aim to have three to five stories that you can more or less memorize (without sounding too scripted) and adapt them to the context of specific interview questions.

3. Google lists of behavioral questions. They should look and sound roughly like those listed above. Practice (ideally with a partner) responding to the questions by adapting your stories to the nature of the questions you're asked. Try not to sound too scripted! Building fluency in responding to these types of questions will take you from ineptitude to sounding natural and confident.

Behavioral questions are also a really great way to highlight your PM Superpower (Chapter 6). When given the opportunity, talk about the unique value you would bring (or have brought) to these scenarios; this will highlight your potential future contributions to their organization.

Some of the really interesting interview processes will apply their own touches to behavioral interview questions. For example, companies with publicly available core values will often try to assess, from a candidate's responses to behavioral questions, how closely they align with those values. Audible (the audiobook division of

Amazon, which was acquired in 2008) retains core values independent of its parent organization and expects its new hires to live those values in the way that they approach their work. In such situations, a candidate should map his stories to the values of the target company and rigorously practice his responses to questions specifically about how he's demonstrated those values in the workplace.

Of course, culture can be evaluated in many ways outside of behavioral questions, as well. Be prepared to speak to your personal interests, industry news or recent broader changes in the tech space. Research your interviewers on LinkedIn, their personal websites, blog posts they've written, and whatever else you can find in order to identify topics of discussion. This can be a great way to impress. At the end of the day, you're selling something (yourself) and you should do whatever you can reasonably and ethically do in order to close that deal.

Bringing your authentic self (Braxton)

A value I hold dear, possibly dearest, is authenticity. As a candidate, I don't try to sugarcoat any mistakes I've made or any personal attributes that may not be a fit for a company's culture but instead lay my cards on the table and hope that the hiring team will appreciate my candor and humility. If some aspect of my personality or working style isn't the right fit, it's probably better for both sides if we don't waste any more of each other's time.

Recently, in my role as a hiring manager, a candidate was exceptionally transparent about his background as a "wayward youth" and how he found his personal path, values, and experiences in a way that gave me more confidence about him throughout his process with us. He impressed our team with his technical knowledge and approach but just as important was his thoughtfulness and honesty, which were especially important to our founders. Although this candidate had received two other offers on the same day that we decided to hire him, he leveled with us (and vice versa) such that we were able to construct an offer that was appropriate for our company and compelling to him. Increasingly, in Product, the nice human finishes first.

PART 3

Landing the Job

CHAPTER 12

Breaking into Product Management for the First Time

Let's take a moment to recap what we have covered so far in *Product Sense*.

First, we took a close look at the fundamentals one would need in order to be acknowledged as an industry-agnostic PM. From there, we learned how to strategically approach the WSB Problem ("What should we build, and why?"), the cornerstone of your day-to-day life in Product. Most recently, we learned about the Compass Framework, which is a tool that can be utilized to answer PM case questions (in which you essentially solve the WSB problem for a specific product) during a PM interview.

What now?

The next chapters will focus on the logistics of searching for a job in Product.

- We'll start by discussing how to break into Product for the very first time.

- Next, we'll explore a framework designed to help you identify your target company and land an interview.

- We'll then walk you through how to maximize your odds of a successful interview by properly preparing ahead of time.

- Finally, we will map out what the experience of applying and interviewing is actually like—to give you a real sense of the process—so you'll know what to expect.

Whether you are making a career shift but haven't interviewed in a few years *or* are brand new to Product, this part of the book will give you the latest methods and the most cutting-edge tips to help you navigate what might otherwise be a very intimidating process.

Let's begin with the story of Janet, a PM we interviewed when writing this book.

Janet's Story

Janet was a senior at the University of Minnesota majoring in Chemistry. As Janet's graduation date approached, she decided to look for a job in Silicon Valley. Growing up, her family members often turned to her for "IT support." Thus, they were not surprised to see her contemplating a career in tech.

Janet received and accepted an offer for a customer support role at an insurance tech company in Menlo Park. The job was a great opportunity in its own right, as well as a stepping stone (she hoped) toward a more senior leadership position.

Janet soon became a critical member of the customer support team, which gave her a special vantage point within the company. As a provider of frontline support for customer needs, Janet dealt with customer problems and issues on a daily basis. She quickly noticed that many customers complained about very basic issues (seemingly due to difficulties with understanding how to use the product) that should have been avoided or solved by the product's onboarding sequence or tutorials.

Using her own product sense, Janet deduced that there was an insufficient self-serve experience for many of the company's customers. She knew that, as sometimes happens in B2B companies, most of the attention and resources were being focused on the firm's large, enterprise clients—while the smaller clients (often without a direct line to an account manager) were being neglected and relegated by default to an inadequate, self-managed experience.

Janet quickly developed a reputation as the foremost champion of the self-service user, as well as the subject-matter expert on anything pertaining to onboarding, user experience, and customer engagement. Although she still served in her original customer support role, executives began to notice that she always went above and beyond *and* that she was developing product expertise.

Eventually, Janet had the opportunity to give a presentation to senior leadership. In the presentation, she described how she would change the product to vastly improve the customer experience and illustrated the anticipated impact these improvements would bring to retention, revenue, and other core metrics. The company's leadership was very impressed and Janet soon found herself on the Product team as a PM, tasked with overseeing and improving the customer experience.

Janet had broken into product management.

People often refer to getting their first PM job as "breaking into Product" because it can be very difficult to make this leap. Many PM job descriptions list "X years of product management experience" as a prerequisite to being invited to interview, so first-time PM candidates face a classic chicken-and-egg scenario: How can one accumulate PM experience if every PM job requires such experience before you can interview for said job?

If you are not sure where to begin to get your *first* job in product management, this chapter is for you. Just like Janet (and many other PMs we spoke to while researching this book), you *can* successfully break into Product and secure your dream job as a PM. This chapter will cover several strategies that you can use to make this dream come true.

Overcoming the Experience Gap

A lack of direct Product experience might make obtaining a job as a PM seem impossible. "They only want experienced PMs," a disheartened candidate might say.

Changing your mindset will help free you from this limiting belief and push you forward. In product management, imposter syndrome (feeling that you might not have what it takes to be considered for a PM role or even the ability to do the PM job that you already have) is very real and many of us experience it at some point. Even PMs who are trying to make a lateral or upwards move in Product report feeling this way at times, since the PM interview process can be quite daunting.

It's important to keep in mind that there is no clearly defined path to working in Product and that few people have formal product management education—there are, quite simply, very few available programs or classes and their value is questionable. The best preparation includes developing your product sense, understanding the process, and presenting yourself as a good culture fit and a relentless problem solver.

In researching this book, we learned that experienced PMs looking for a new job sometimes feel like they are out of practice or that they might not cut it at another organization. One thing to keep in mind is that a PM is not a commodity. Each PM's experience, problem-solving capabilities, and outlook on the world is unique. As a PM or a future PM, you'll be looking for a Product team that is a good match for *you* and the skills and attitude that you can bring to the table.

Our aim in writing this book is to help you break through the "experience wall" with confidence, and with the belief that your background is valuable and that you are right for the job. It is absolutely possible to leverage your previous work and make a case as to why you are the best candidate for a PM role. The key is to present yourself so that you, and your talents, stand out to your interviewers.

Finding Your Way into Product

What might feel like a large leap into Product can actually be achieved in two smaller hops.

First, it's best if you are coming from a role that is in some way tangential to product management. Second, you will need to seek out ways to demonstrate that you possess product-related skills.

Imagine the challenge that hiring managers face when searching for someone to fill a role on their team. It's often a case of information asymmetry. While you might know that you would excel at the job, they do not know this. As we said earlier, there are no degrees specifically in product management and it can be difficult to exhibit your skill set clearly during the recruitment process. You need to make sure that your potential value as a PM cannot possibly be missed.

Managers desperately want to avoid a bad hire because the cost of a "false positive" is extraordinarily high. In addition to the operational costs of hiring someone who doesn't work out (for example, time spent onboarding new employees), the recruiting process must be restarted and represents substantial **opportunity cost.** The hiring manager needs to be sure that the candidate will be able to handle the day-to-day aspects of the role she will fill. This obligates the hiring team to be highly demanding during the interview process, which can take weeks or even months for some of the most elusive roles. So let's break down the aforementioned "two hops" to gauge where you currently are in the Product game.

Hop #1: Are You Already in a Tangential Role?

By working in a role that is *tangential,* or in some way peripheral, to a Product team, you should (at least in theory) already be familiar with what a PM contributes from day to day within an organization. A tangential role is most commonly one of the cross-functional partners, which include (but are not limited to) design, marketing, and engineering. From a nontech perspective, finance and management consultants sometimes gravitate to PM roles, and can fit in quite nicely.

Here is a brief chart of some tangential roles, commonly found in technology organizations, and why they can lead to a career in product management.

Role	Skills/experience that translate to PM
Product Marketing	Strong communication skills, collaborates with many departments, already works with the Product team, comfortable analyzing data
Customer Acquisition	Has a developed understanding of and empathy for the customer, comfortable analyzing data
Growth	Skill set includes focusing on metrics commonly used by the Product team, may already work with the designers and developers, may have experience designing A/B tests
Customer Support	Brings a deep understanding of both customer and product to the table, great communications skills, customer empathy
Sales	Brings an understanding of broader industry trends and competitor offerings, communication skills

Contributing to a team in one of these capacities will almost certainly give you a leg up when applying for a Product role or trying to transition into one. If you don't necessarily fall into any of these buckets, consider spending some time in one of these roles first. Alternatively, one or more of the strategies we will outline later may apply to your current circumstances and become your "secret sauce" during the product management recruiting process. At the end of the day, what's most important is to craft a narrative that highlights your capabilities and articulates your desire to succeed in a product management role.

Hop #2: Demonstrate Your Product Sense Attributes

Now, let's assume that you have been exposed to Product teams in some capacity while working in one of the roles that we just discussed. Your next step is to prove yourself as a potential Product leader by exhibiting the product sense *attributes* that will help you stand out within your company, or from a pile of resumes.

It's important to identify a pathway to follow as you transition yourself from where you are now, into the role of a PM. To help you, we have outlined five pathways that others have used to do just this. For each, we have also highlighted a *product sense attribute* that can (and should!) be leveraged in each one. As you read on, consider which of these scenarios might be the right for you. Your personal narrative, celebrating what makes you unique, and selecting the right companies to aim for will all be aspects of your overarching strategy (we will touch on selecting the right role at the right company in the following chapter).

Pathway #1: An internal transition to PM

As you learned from reading Janet's story, a prime example of breaking into product management is via an internal transfer. In such cases, a prospective PM has had an opportunity to demonstrate that she would be a great fit for the Product team. If this circumstance applies to you, perhaps your coworkers and current manager would be willing to advocate for you (assuming that they support your transfer). Even if your manager does not support your desire to move into a PM role, you can still network internally with PMs or other team leaders who may help you build your case.

Deeply understanding the problem space and users is a valuable feather in your cap. Perhaps, like Janet, you have worked in customer service and have firsthand knowledge of the issues that users have faced with the product, as well as their suggested solutions. Another advantage might exist if you are known for consistent and reliable execution. As in many other aspects of life, opportunities often arise based on who you know. Any existing, positive relationships or allies you may have on the Product teams you are thinking of joining will often prove to be invaluable.

The key to transferring internally is to demonstrate that you understand the product extensively and, more importantly, the customer problems that need to be solved in order to make the product even more successful.

For example, if you are coming from Sales, you might argue that your experience working on the front lines and directly interacting with customers makes you an attractive new teammate. With your finger on the pulse of new client prospects—many of whom are trying to choose between your product and that of your competitors—you could bring to the Product team ideas for compelling new features that would differentiate your product and elevate it within the market. **Use your existing role as a selling point**. Remember, your experience is unique and valuable and the Product team cannot find anyone else like you!

The process of an internal transfer into Product will differ vastly from company to company. Sometimes it's easy, other times it is not. Henry, another subject whom we interviewed for *Product Sense*, had a more complicated journey.

For several years, Henry was a member of a business analysis team at a FAANG company. At this particular firm, it appeared (to him) that members of Product teams had the best career opportunities—PMs seemed to have clear progression, more influence on the company and product strategy, and excellent reputations within the tech industry.

In Henry's case, his company had developed a formal process for internal transfers into Product. However, a successful transfer was by no means guaranteed, even if the candidate had a tremendous track record. There were rumors that, in some instances, those attempting an internal transfer seemed to have more difficulty securing PM roles than the external applicants. Peer reviews and performance check-ins meant that an employee was a "known quantity" with respect to skill set and other qualities, and the company could tell more easily who was qualified for certain role changes. Henry relayed to us, in fact, that some peers had resorted to leaving the company, becoming PMs elsewhere, and subsequently returning to the company with the credentials required to claim a PM role.

Obviously, Henry had several hurdles to overcome. First, he needed a Product Lead (a PM that manages a team of other PMs) to approve him to shadow his or her Product team and observe their decision-making process. This meant that he would effectively be working two jobs concurrently. While he shadowed the Product team, and occasionally engaged in discussions with the Lead, the PM team developed a sense of Henry's problem-solving skills and overall product sense. Henry hoped that the Product Lead would decide that there was a potential fit for him within that team and product area.

If this happened, then Henry would advance to the next step in the process. Luckily for him, he was able to move forward!

Henry's second step was to obtain approval from both a manager and a Vice President, to continue pursuing a move to Product. In some companies, this step is just a formality but, in others, it can be a major blocker (if, for instance, the employee previously made some highly visible gaffe). Thankfully, Henry was a solid contributor in good standing and without any skeletons in his closet!

As a final step, Henry had to navigate the same interview loop that an external candidate would. His interviewers—people he had known and worked with in his time with the company—were asked to give unbiased assessments of his performance during one-hour blocks of case questions. Henry did his best to answer the case questions and show his product knowledge, skill sets, and potential value if given the chance to make this internal move. In the end, an offer was not extended. While this was hard for Henry, his interviewers were supportive and shared some feedback on his interview performance along with suggested areas to improve—far more so than if he had been an external candidate.

When speaking to us about this experience, Henry shared what he would have done differently. First, he would have spent more time upfront establishing relationships with the Product team he was interested in joining: gaining allies and building support. Second, he would have prepared more thoroughly; he mistakenly assumed that interviewing at his own company would be easier than doing so elsewhere. However, it can be just as difficult, or even more so, to change disciplines within a company than for an outside hire to secure the same role.

Pathway #2: Rotational product manager programs and internships

As a means to attract young product managers who can grow into future leaders, rotational product manager programs ("RPMs") have become increasingly popular at large organizations as a means to attract young product managers who can grow into future leaders over time. Such programs are often a good option, especially for someone who is nearing graduation from an undergraduate or graduate program, or is at an earlier stage in their career.

In a rotational program, recruits participate in a curriculum designed to expose them to different parts of the company's business. The aim may be to groom promising candidates for a career in, say, Product, but the candidates need have no previous experience in this area. Facebook's RPM consists of three six-month rotations (each segment spent on a different product team). The program's website notes that its mission "is to develop future Product leaders by empowering, mentoring, and enabling them to build and learn across a variety of products across Facebook." The focus is on recruiting junior staffers and developing them over an eighteen-month period.

The benefits to the employer are twofold. First, the company has a larger set of candidates from which it can draw. If you are solely focused on hiring experienced PMs, the candidate pool is smaller. Young and bright people with the right mindsets can be developed into great PMs. There are the costs of running these programs, of course, but the organizations maintaining them are, in general, quite large and can afford to risk bringing on recruits who *don't* work out in order to find the few that *do*.

The second benefit is that such programs cultivate generalist PMs—meaning that graduates have solid fundamental product management skills, as well as domain expertise, after being exposed to different areas of the company and many strong Product leaders. Thus, lateral movement between different teams is easier and the company enjoys higher PM retention. Fewer PMs choose to leave the organization, and fewer team mismatches occur.

Rotational programs bear some similarities to formal internship programs, which are also common at larger companies. A major difference between the two is that internships typically last only about three months. Seldom can an individual with no PM experience ramp up and complete meaningful Product work in such a short period of time. The goal of an internship, for the company, is to potentially hire one or more interns as full-time PMs the following year.

If you complete an internship but do not ultimately receive a job offer, you have still gained PM experience that, on a resume and as part of your professional narrative, can be an asset when interviewing with other companies. Receiving an offer at the end of an internship is never a given, for various reasons, whereas the RPMs are full-time employees who are trained by, and allowed to explore, different Product teams across the company.

PM Rotational Programs versus Internships		
	Length of Program	*Benefits*
Internship	3 months	Resume builder, potential to receive a full-time offer, meaningful introduction to product management
RPM	12–18 months	In-depth and diverse experience, exposure to a variety of teams/roles, job security

We spoke with several hiring managers for APM/RPM programs. (APMs are associate product manager programs, such as Google's program which consists of two one-year rotations.) By all accounts, the selection process for these programs is highly competitive. Generally, the programs recruit from top universities and also have a large applicant pool of recent grads. The bar during the interview process is similar to that expected of industry hires who are further along in their careers. If you are targeting one of these programs, you should prepare for your interviews using our guidance throughout *Product Sense*. One aspiring PM we spoke to shared these thoughts after completing a rotational program interview loop at a FAANG company:

> *"It's an awesome opportunity for someone new to the PM space, because it gives the necessary depth and breadth to maximize impact and growth. I heard that the RPM program really pushes you to bring out your best self, and you have real ownership of products, but your experience might differ depending on the lifecycle of the Product team you join.*
>
> *A myth about these programs, though, is their bias for candidates from top schools. Based on many of the profiles you*

come across, this could prove to be true, but it definitely wouldn't stop you from getting that interview. I would say that graduating from a top school or having work experience at a well-known company would definitely set you apart and increase your chances of landing that offer but it wouldn't guarantee it. Another common theme among RPMs is that they are usually people with some form of entrepreneurship, consulting, civic backgrounds or prior PM experience. But each class has diverse candidates, so leverage what makes you unique!

These programs are very competitive and it would be nice to get in, but I'd say do not put all of your eggs in one basket. Seek other great PM opportunities. Due to the small size of the rotational programs, there are hundreds of equally talented candidates that will get rejected—but that shouldn't deter you from reapplying in the future if you still feel connected to the opportunity or organization. Product Management is a growing field and each day there are more opportunities and new companies seeking this expertise. Every company is becoming a tech company! Also, do not get discouraged or beat yourself up because you didn't get invited for interviews for these programs. Their rejection most likely does not mean you are not a qualified, high-potential PM. They have their selection criteria plus they receive tens of thousands of applications. It is competitive!

—Uche Ekeopara,
Master of Engineering Management, Class of 2021

Pathway #3: Domain expertise

In order to understand how becoming a domain expert can help you land a PM job, it's important to first step back and consider the PM recruitment process. Broadly speaking, there are two approaches to PM recruitment: hiring generalists or hiring specialists.

Generalists come with across-the-board fundamental PM skills and can apply those fundamentals in order to manage many different types of product areas. As we mentioned in Pathway #2, larger companies tend to lean toward hiring generalists as they scale. Perhaps you are reading *Product Sense* because you are preparing to interview with this type of company. If so, our guidance should help set you up for success. However, the rule is not hard and fast. Even larger companies might have roles that require a certain kind of expertise, or a specialized team that needs someone who can hit the ground running on day one.

Smaller companies more often want to hire someone who will tell *them* what to do, rather than the other way around; this type of hire might be considered a specialist role since the hire will bring deep subject-matter expertise to the table.

Domain expertise comes in many forms. For instance, perhaps a team is building a product for a very specific type of user and you happen to have a unique and deep understanding of this particular user's needs and problems. Here are some more examples:

- A streaming platform may want to hire someone who has been involved with the eSports community (the PM is already immersed in the community and has relationships with and understanding of the primary users and content generators).

- A video-hosting service may want to hire the author of a long-running vlog (the vlog author already knows which tools content creators need).

- A popular gaming company may want to hire a PM with deep knowledge of game mechanics (this type of PM knows what makes a game fun).

- A social-networking company may want to hire someone who has created AR content (this hire can help enable a strategic pivot into that space).

- A developer-tools company may want to hire someone who has sourced and evaluated enterprise software (this hire will help them best adhere to compliance measures).

If you are familiar with the industry in which a company operates, you can effectively and efficiently manage day-to-day responsibilities with minimal onboarding.

If this pathway is an option for you, highlight your qualifying attributes on your resume and also include them in the narrative that you convey to recruiters and hiring managers. If you can leverage other tactics to demonstrate your knowledge (i.e., writing about it on Medium or in a personal blog), you should do so. Becoming an expert in a space becomes a nice hook since you are already familiar with the industry shifts and customer pain points. Even if you are not interested in working in a given sector for the long term, you will still accumulate valuable PM experience while you are there. Then, if you have a command of general PM fundamentals, you can transition into another company or industry later on.

Passion for The Industry (Peter)

My first PM job, at Zynga, was a result of a passion for the games industry. As you might remember from my bio in the Introduction, games had been a large part of my life and I wanted to get into the industry. I learned everything I could about social games, what key metrics were important, what the best developers were doing, and what "good" looked like. This research and passion paid off, I was offered an PM internship during my last summer in college, in a cohort of PMs that were all MBAs. That internship converted to a full-time job beginning the following year. If you do the heavy lifting to become knowledgeable about your target industry, you will be competent and coherent when you interview, giving you the best chance at success.

Pathway #4: Side project or startup

Several of the PMs we spoke to while writing this book shared that they broke into product management, in part, by using a side project or small startup to showcase their abilities and interests. This pathway, while viable, is contingent upon the depth of the acquired experience and your ability to clearly communicate the impact you were able to deliver through your efforts.

For example, launching a project from start to finish (i.e., from **zero to one**) shows that you are able to manage and execute on a project all the way up to and across the finish line, or at least through a major milestone. Additionally, communicating your results gives you an opportunity to demonstrate PM vocabulary and structured thinking. Articulating your impact in a measurable way allows the hiring manager to draw parallels between what you have achieved and the requirements for the PM role for which she is hiring. Crafting a compelling narrative around this experience signals to the hiring manager in no uncertain terms that you can get stuff done and deliver results!

Pathway #5: Business school

Employers hiring PMs may list an MBA in either the requirements or the "nice-to-have" sections of a job description. The truth, however, is that MBAs are almost never *required* for Product roles. In an article that Peter wrote in 2017 analyzing hundreds of PM job postings, he discovered that "MBA" only appeared in the requirements section about two percent of the time.

In practice, you will find that many PMs do have MBAs. For example, some professionals pursue MBA degrees when considering early- or mid-career transitions. Those who start their careers in a discipline such as finance or consulting may decide to move into the tech sector and will use the full-time, two-year MBA program as a way to broaden their skill sets and explore their next moves.

Some companies prefer to recruit MBAs as summer interns after their first year in graduate programs, likely because they have some years of work experience whereas most undergraduate interns have none. This isn't a hard and fast rule; in fact, while the authors of this book first met in an intern cohort consisting mostly of MBA students, Braxton already had his MBA, while Peter had just finished his junior year of college.

An MBA can help (Braxton)

My decision to pursue an MBA at Columbia Business School resulted in one of the most impactful experiences of my life. I began my career in public accounting, followed by a stint leading a small process and internal controls function at the USO. Although I enjoyed aspects of my job, especially international travel, my progression was limited and I didn't feel at home in the culture of accounting and finance teams. I was incredibly fortunate to be admitted to CBS, where I was exposed to many new career paths, internships and full-time opportunities, and had a once-in-a-lifetime chance to make many new friends and contacts within the program. I may have been able to break into tech with my pre-MBA background but it would have been extremely difficult given my lack of West Coast connections or experience. Product management would almost certainly have *initially* been out of reach. Also, I was able to approximately double my pre-MBA compensation. For a relatively young person reading this book, a top-tier MBA should be on the table as a pathway into PM.

Non-MBA experience (Peter)

I have a different point of view on this than Braxton does. Fortunately for me, my passion for gaming and knowledge of that industry (from an internship during college) landed me a full-time job after completing my undergraduate degree. This was a domain expertise (well, passion) path into PM. After getting into Product, I noticed that throughout my career my upward progression (e.g., promotions, raises) was on par with my peers with MBAs. Once you are working in product management, no benefits of MBA exist from what I have seen. I did some analysis and wrote in a blog post about this, but an MBA is hardly ever listed as a requirement for a PM role. Not everyone has the financial freedom or time investment available for them to become a full-time student again. That's fine—you can land a PM job by being a person with a well-honed product sense, combined with passion for the industry.

That said, if business school makes sense for your personal circumstances, it almost certainly won't hurt your prospects in the Product world. However, more important than an MBA are your years of experience in a related field, domain knowledge, clear passion for the product, and the general understanding of how to develop products.

Summing It Up

As we've mentioned before, you will hear the phrase "breaking into product management" often when exploring whether this field is for you. *Product Sense* was born out of the belief that the transition into Product doesn't have to be a black box. The pathways outlined in this chapter should give you a solid understanding of how to convey that you are or could be a great PM.

Hopefully, after reading up to this point, you now possess the skill set and mindset necessary to tackle the job. All of your experiences are valuable and given that PMs come in many different flavors, there is sure to be a PM role out there that is tailor made just for you. The key is to remember your narrative and your superpower, play to your strengths, and pick a pathway that makes the most sense for your situation.

CHAPTER 13

Finding (and Landing) the Job: From Start to Finish

The PM interview process itself can be daunting, exhausting, and lengthy, based on the idiosyncrasies of the opportunities that you pursue. On the other hand, we'd like you to try to frame it as a great learning experience, a way to meet new people, a personal challenge, and a chance to evaluate whether a particular job might be right for you. Fit is a two-way street.

The Job Search Process

Here is a look at what we'll cover in this chapter. We will do our best to detail the steps you may (and most likely will) face as you kick off the recruiting process.

1. Selecting your target company
2. Tuning your resume
3. The recruiter screen
4. The take-home product exercise
5. Onsite interviews
6. Accepting an offer (and dealing with rejection)

Depending on the size of the organization, or the structure of a particular team, you'll notice differences in interview composition and possibly even sequence. However, across the board you should be prepared to spend at least six to eight hours getting to know folks within the team and organization—as you speak to your many different experiences and skills—while they seek to assess your fit for the role.

Step 1: Selecting Target Companies

The first step toward landing a PM job is to find companies that fit your profile *and* have open roles. There are so many different types of products, teams, and industries that finding the right matches for you may feel a little like looking for needles in haystacks.

Selecting your target company is a vital step when beginning your job search, because it impacts how you will tackle the preparation process. Applying to hundreds of jobs at once is a recipe for disappointment. A more targeted, structured approach will yield you the best result. Think a dozen or so, not hundreds. Careful examination of what is really important to you in a PM job (your personal North Star!), will point you to the best job openings for you—the ones that will allow you to continue to grow your career, offer a path to leadership positions, and involve you in exciting projects with like-minded peers.

You'll see the term "target company" used repeatedly in the following sections. A target company is a specific organization you will choose as the focus of your efforts and to which you will submit an application. As you develop your resume, your narrative, and your superpower story—and especially as you prepare to handle PM case questions in an interview setting—you will tailor all of these elements to your target company.

Where to begin

We spend many of our waking hours working. In writing this book, and reflecting on our years as PMs, it's become clear to us that Product is our passion. Somewhere along the line we became drawn to the challenges of being PMs, and we love what we do. That's not to say that every moment of our professional lives has been riveting . . . every job has its mundane aspects and bad days. Nevertheless, we've found product management to be an incredibly dynamic discipline that engages our intellectual curiosity and fulfills our desire to work with others to build something great.

In the next few pages, we'll provide some perspective on different company types and place them into "buckets of interest" for candidates to consider. While this will give you a great starting point, there are a few other factors that might help to increase your odds of finding a position that is personally and professionally rewarding. For example:

- What are your personal interests? Do you like gadgets? Perhaps something related to software for phones, tablets, or smart devices interests you. Or maybe you care about climate change and a company promoting alternative energy needs a new PM. Do politics rock your world? You might consider working at a think tank or on a presidential or senatorial campaign. By identifying your interests, you will likely find that you are already halfway to the PM role of your dreams. Your humble authors both found their first PM roles at gaming companies because gaming was important in their personal lives. What is important to you?

- Do you have friends or acquaintances who already work for a company you are interested in? If you feel that working with friends is important, is there an opening on their team or within the same firm? From the authors' earliest days in Product, relationships forged at work have contributed to our personal and professional happiness—and often far outlasted our time at the jobs where they began. This book is the product of a friendship which began in the workplace!

Selecting your company

Since we started working in Product, the discipline has garnered substantially more attention and mainstream appeal. Many factors have contributed to this phenomenon but several immediately come to mind:

1. General growth of the tech sector in the U.S. and world economy (especially big tech)

2. Migration of product managers trained within big tech (e.g., Google, Amazon, Facebook, Zynga) to senior roles in medium and small tech companies, who subsequently built out full-fledged Product teams

3. Propensity of former tech PMs to found their own companies and subsequently hire their own PMs

4. Demystification of the product manager role due to greater availability of resources and literature

5. Appearance of the CPO (Chief Product Officer), which has elevated Product to C-Level

All of these reasons, among others, have contributed to a surge in available Product positions at firms in the United States and around the world. This, in turn, has attracted the attention of thousands of MBA graduates, former consultants, marketers, engineers, and others—all seeking to change paths within the scope of Product.

The table below outlines the main types of companies a PM might work for, along with examples of each, arranged by company size.

Company Type	Examples	Company Size
Big Tech	Amazon, Google, Facebook, Netflix, Microsoft, Salesforce, Airbnb, Spotify, Uber, Lyft	Very large
Traditional Corporations	General Electric, Morgan Stanley, Dell, Oracle, IBM	Large
Consulting Firms	McKinsey, Bain, BCG, Deloitte, Accenture	Medium to large
Established Startups	Betterment, Duolingo, MasterClass, Coinbase	Varies significantly
New Ventures (Early-Stage Startups)	N/A	Very small

By no means is this table meant to be exhaustive. In fact, there may very well be other types of product management roles that you will come across in your professional experience or job search. For example, some nonprofits have begun to hire product managers to work on digital initiatives. Nevertheless, we believe that the list above includes some of the most typical and numerous opportunities.

In terms of picking a company, it is generally advisable to be more targeted in your approach, as opposed to going very wide. If your goal is to learn product management from the best in the industry, and you want more room for lateral movement (the ability to change teams within your company, when desired), your best bet may be to shoot for one of the bigger tech companies. That might come with a bit of a smaller scope, however, as product teams in FAANG and related companies tend to work on more narrow assignments. If you envision yourself wearing many hats and owning a larger scope project, perhaps a startup would be more your size. In any case, excitement for the industry or problem space should be an important consideration as you search.

Differences in company types

Product management can also vary by the size and maturity of the company. Although the exact role of a PM tends not to be quite the same in any two companies, we've attempted to break down some common types of opportunities that you might find, as well as what product management might roughly look like in each of these spaces.

Big Tech

We have used the term FAANG throughout this book. As a refresher, this term represents a set of large, publicly held, tech companies (Facebook, Amazon, Apple, Netflix, and Google), whose combined valuation in September of 2020 reached approximately $6 trillion. These entities have driven profoundly transformative change in the last twenty or so years—impacting the very way we live our lives. As they have grown, they have had a significant influence on how modern product management is practiced. Alumni from these firms can be found in C-suites in many smaller tech firms and startups, venture capital firms, and on corporate boards.

It should come as no surprise that FAANG companies and a handful of other large players hire large numbers of PMs. In fact, dozens of graduates from each of the top MBA programs make their way straight to FAANG Product teams, especially at Amazon! Although there are many open roles, the process required to land one tends to be quite competitive, since these companies are so widely known. Hopeful candidates are subjected to rigorous interview loops, complete with case and behavioral questions, to help ensure that the company is screening for and hiring only the best talent. Employees often receive high base salaries and meaningful equity compensation, as well as amazing benefits and office perks.

A typical PM and product team in a big tech company would likely look like this:

- **The PM Role:**
    - Smaller sphere of product ownership
    - A more structured approach to product management and **agile development**
    - Access to best-in-class proprietary analytics, deployment, and experimentation tools
    - Clear career progression and strong resume-building opportunities due to high recognition and positive external perception of big tech brands
    - Excellent compensation, including large salary and some equity
- **The Product Team:**
    - Collaboration with many top-tier, experienced Product leaders and peers

- Large, highly talented engineering organization with which to partner

Established startups

Working for a startup can be an outstanding opportunity for a product manager. A "startup" is traditionally thought of as a newly established business, but the rapid pace of the technology sector has blurred this definition a bit. In some cases, companies that are ten years old, relatively small, and not public would be considered startups. However, some slightly younger companies have grown and evolved to such a degree that they are now more appropriately considered Big Tech (e.g., Airbnb).

As you think about where you might want to work as a product manager, you should also evaluate where your target companies are in their life cycles. As we just noted, some of today's startups will evolve into tomorrow's Big Tech (or be acquired by it!). Startups tend to be earlier in their life cycles than Big Tech, as reflected by less mature processes, fewer institutional learnings, and the extent to which they've "figured out" their space and product-market fit. These characteristics excite certain types of PMs and prospective PMs and, consequently, a startup can be a great fit for them—if there is a position in Product available.

For example, a new product manager might be able to turn some consulting or previous tech experience into a Director of Product role at a startup, operating in a space where that individual has some domain expertise or where their project management, polish, and people management skills are desired.

An important part of evaluating product management opportunities at a startup will be to understand the startup's current size, history, and funding (i.e., how much cash it has in the bank and how quickly it is drawing down those reserves, since many startups are not profitable), and its overall growth and momentum. This will help you to better understand the risk that you personally might be taking by joining a particular startup. Joining a startup, even a large and well established one, almost always carries more risk than Big Tech. Not all of the information noted here will be readily available to you, but it will be well worth your time to ferret out as much as you can.

A startup product management organization might look like this:

- **The PM Role:**
  - Larger sphere of product ownership, potentially the entirety of the product
  - Limited tools, usually some off-the-shelf software (e.g., Optimizely for experimentation, Looker/Mixpanel/Amplitude for analytics)
  - Lack of formal processes and/or commitment to a typical way of doing things, but the opportunity to help shape the organization's evolution
  - Lack of clarity around career progression (i.e., chart your own course)
  - Compensation can vary drastically—typically less cash but potentially a larger equity share in the company—and with this comes risk!
- **The Product Team:**
  - Smaller, less experienced, and less mature team

- Potentially less experienced and less numerous engineering talent
- Tight-knit cultures in which Product collaborates with all or most parts of the business

Consulting firms

Consulting firms are more recent entrants into the product-manager hiring frenzy. Players such as Deloitte and Accenture have long been in the business of implementing large software platforms as well as customizing existing platforms. These organizations now have numerous opportunities for product managers to partner with engineers, designers, and traditional consultants to help clients solve technology problems and even develop entirely new products.

That said, elite management consulting firms like McKinsey, Bain, and BCG are in the process of staffing up their own implementation teams. These firms recently realized that executing on the guidance served by their generalist consultants requires new skill sets for which they had not previously recruited. In addition to product managers, they are hiring large classes of engineers, designers, and data scientists. Consulting firms are demonstrating, in real time, the global trend of organizing digital efforts to mirror the structures and processes at big tech.

It's worth noting that all of these firms have product managers serving in support functions, as well. For example, they hire their own PMs to help manage customizations for their off-the-shelf and proprietary software tools and platforms, in order to manage vast, distributed workplaces and specialized needs. Additionally, they are acquiring and developing, or even incubating, tools to be used by clients that require product management talent. These PM roles more closely resemble those that you might find at a traditional corporation, which we will discuss next.

In short, these firms have a surprising number of product management roles, some of which may interest you.

Elements of a PM role or product team to consider when looking at consulting firms:

- **The PM Role:**
  - Mix of off-the-shelf and proprietary tools and software
  - For client-facing PMs, typically a clear progression path (similar to generalist consultants)
  - Deep commitment to training and substantial in-house training and professional development resources
  - For client-facing PMs, the possibility of extensive travel (Monday through Thursday, every week)
  - Strong resume-building opportunities due to high recognition and positive external perception of top-tier firms
  - Outstanding compensation and benefits
  - Widespread alumni networks enabling future employment opportunities
- **The Product Team:**
  - Decentralized (or even fragmented) Product organizations
  - Generally less experienced engineering and design teams

Traditional corporations

There are many established corporations (think IBM, General Electric, consumer packaged goods companies, General Motors, and many more) that build digital products as part of their core businesses or create proprietary internal digital products and platforms to support their large and diverse workforces. These companies can sometimes offer very interesting opportunities for product managers.

Although they might not be as flashy as Big Tech, great opportunities abound within these behemoths and they are worth a look by nearly anyone in Product. Rather than hiring large classes of PMs and training them, they more commonly look for experienced professionals with specialized skill sets or particular domain knowledge.

In a traditional corporate setting, PMs and product teams may look something like this:

- **The PM Role:**
    - Depending on seniority, potentially clear progression (due to organizational hierarchy)
    - Good or excellent compensation and benefits
    - Off-the-shelf tools and platforms
    - Potentially interesting internal transfers and new project opportunities
    - In-house training or training budgets
    - Good brand association and resume-building opportunities

- More likely to exhibit a formal environment that *could* lead to potential project stagnation or entanglement in corporate "red tape"
- **The Product Team:**
  - Outstanding internal and external networks
  - Quality of design and engineering talent varies

New ventures (early-stage startups)

For experienced PMs, early-stage startups with only a handful of employees can be a chance to whet their entrepreneurial appetites and boldly go where no PM has gone before. Although these opportunities may look and sound exciting, be warned that most early-stage startups (as in, upwards of ninety percent) fail, and you may soon find yourself on the job market again. If the company doesn't survive long enough for its product to find traction and to define a viable business model, you may have nothing to show for your efforts.

There's something else that you should know ... you will be working very closely with the founders, owners, or creators of the company, and they will be heavily invested in the company's success. Because they care so deeply, and desperately want to nurture and protect their company, they may have little tolerance for error or even the ability or willingness to offer you much time to find your footing. We cannot emphasize this enough: rapport with the founding team is important to establish but may be difficult to achieve.

On the other hand, if you are able to quickly establish trust and strong relationships with the founding team (or at least accomplish being viewed as an ally and valuable asset), you may make friends and/or business partners for life. As wonderful as that sounds, a ruthless founder won't let a PM he or she doesn't respect sit in the role for long. You can easily be eliminated, even if it's not personal!

So what might a PM role or Product team look like within a new venture company?

- **The PM Role:**
  - Off-the-shelf tools and platforms (or, literally none—you may have to evaluate and put in place analytics, workflow, or other tools to help you and your team do their jobs)
  - Undefined or limited Product roadmap
  - Lack of formal policies and procedures
  - Very senior (SVP, VP, CPO) title or clear path to seniority
  - Long hours and severely limited time off
  - High risk that enterprise will fail (keep other options open!)
  - Below-market cash compensation but a substantial equity stake
- **The Product Team:**
  - Very small and tight-knit culture
  - Close partnerships with founders/executive leaders
  - Limited personnel (prepare to roll up your sleeves!)

Tailoring your approach, based on the company size or industry, will put you in the best light with the hiring manager and give you a good chance of advancing through the interview process, and/or receiving an offer.

Differences in hiring strategies

Obviously, your experience interviewing for a product management role will vary considerably based on the companies you choose to pursue and the individuals you encounter during the process. Every individual recruiter, interviewer, and hiring manager will inevitably put their own spin on the questions they'll ask and be guilty of some bias in how they ultimately receive and rate you as a candidate.

More established, larger companies (such as FAANG companies) attempt to reduce biases in the interview process by creating structure and using specialized scoring rubrics to evaluate traits that they feel are important preconditions for success within their organizations. For example, interviewers might consider how well the candidate illustrates that his mindset is congruent with key company values (e.g., "demonstrates a data-driven approach to problem solving" or "exhibits 'fail-fast-and-iterate' traits").

Nestled among the different types of companies and Product teams are often certain fundamental differences in hiring philosophies. More stringent hiring criteria might be reflective of how complex the organization is in terms of their product lines, users, and revenue. For example, larger companies may have more PMs because a one-percent increase in revenue is very meaningful and the work that PMs do to optimize products can easily drive incremental growth. We've outlined a few common hiring philosophies below.

- **Precise Hire:** A specific engineering team working on an isolated part of the business (such as billing, data and machine learning, or infrastructure) needs a PM to help balance priorities but also seeks a *specific* skill that fits the team dynamic. This approach is more common in niche areas within larger companies.

- **General Focus Area:** The hiring organization wants a person who has industry experience such that he or she can hit the ground running without a lot of "ramp-up" time. For example, a company might be seeking "fintech" or "development tools" experience. One might encounter this approach in startups that need or want someone with relevant experience to show them the way, because they understand that building a Product culture is an important part of the next step in company growth.

- **Generalists**: More and more companies are building PM teams using this method. A generalist approach means that—regardless of previous experience—the teams test candidates on product management fundamentals, mindset, and leadership abilities. FAANG companies almost exclusively recruit this way, casting a wider net with respect to locating talent, providing clear criteria for evaluating and promoting individuals, and improving employee retention due to easy lateral movements between teams. It is the "liberal arts" approach to product management.

Understanding the landscape of available PM opportunities and selectively networking, researching, and applying will help ensure that the time you invest will be more fruitful. In all likelihood, you'll also be a more enthusiastic and credible candidate. Once you've narrowed down the list of available opportunities, you can begin to focus on how you'll present yourself throughout the process.

Step 1.5: Create Your Preparation Plan

Whether you are shooting for a complete interview gambit at many different companies, or just focused on a role at a single firm, you'll need to establish an airtight preparation plan. Extensive preparation will help you cover the bases in terms of learning about the industry and company dynamic on which you are focused, being up-to-date on the latest product management best practices, and sufficient reps of mock interviews with partners who will give you honest and constructive feedback.

As with most projects, it will be important to be mindful of how you spend your time, as well as intentional about how you go about executing your plan. Writing down your objectives, in terms of how you will prepare, is crucial to going about this process with confidence.

Most people do not give themselves enough time to prepare for a job interview. Please heed our warning: The more time you can give yourself to prepare, the better. That being said, we understand that you can't always know when the best opportunities are going to surface and you might not always have the luxury of advance notice. So, rather than focusing on a timeline, think of your preparation as more of a checklist.

1. **Work backwards:** When do you envision yourself actually starting a job? This varies wildly from person to person. Some need several months of lead time to finish off current

projects or to acquire vesting equity in their current role. Sometimes roles pop up unexpectedly, so the luxury of copious prep time might not exist. Either way, try to reasonably determine how much time you have or need and then schedule each of the following steps into your calendar.

2. **Research companies:** Spend time looking at each of the companies you'll interview with and take note of the most recent funding rounds, founder vision, current product line, and company history.

3. **Go through the product:** Deconstruct and teardown the products you can access, making note of any pain points, interesting features, or potential improvements that jump out at you. Why was product or feature X built this way? What problems are they solving? You may wish to refer back to Chapter 3, where we talked more about deconstructs.

4. **Hone your PM Superpower story:** Make sure you can confidently and smoothly talk about your unique value and what you can bring to the table that benefits your potential new organization. You may wish to refer back to Chapter 6 for more information.

5. **Research interview questions:** Previous interview questions can be found on sites such as Glassdoor, but you can also craft your own with minimal effort. You may wish to refer to our example questions and responses in Chapter 9.

6. **Work with a friend:** Find a friend who also wants to be a PM; perhaps from your alma mater or someone you

encountered at a tech meetup. It helps to have someone on the journey with you who can, ideally, give you feedback on how you're progressing as you fine-tune your responses to PM case questions. Practice mock interviews together, alternating between the roles of interviewer and interviewee.

When it comes to landing your dream PM role, there's no such thing as too much background work or preparation. Write out your plan at the start and keep yourself accountable along the way.

Step 2: Tuning Your Resume

Now that you have examined industries and company types that may interest you, and identified some jobs to which you want to apply, it's time to get your hands dirty and start applying. Your first step will be to prepare your resume.

You may think that a resume is an artifact of the past that you no longer need to create or update. After all, why would some of the premier tech companies of the world—or scrappy startups with ne'er a printer to be seen during your office tours, for that matter—still require candidates to use a Microsoft Word template and to write out random BS bullet points about their former jobs? While the traditional resume format and content haven't changed much in decades, a proper record of your skills and experience can and does serve a purpose and is often still a necessary part of the job-hunting process.

On most days, it *does* feel like the world is moving beyond the need for resumes. Some of the jobs to which the authors have applied, especially those to which we were referred, have not required resumes. Rather, our friends and former colleagues simply emailed our LinkedIn profiles to the hiring managers or recruiters and that was sufficient to kick off the interviewing process. That said, unless you're being referred for a specific job, you should be prepared to upload your resume or email it to your point of contact when the time comes.

Think of polishing your resume less as a chore and more as a chance to showcase a timeline of your professional accomplishments (because during an interview, you inevitably speak to where you've been, where you are now, and where you're going). A good resume can also help you clarify your memory and understanding of your past experiences so that you can more easily bring them to bear when an interviewer poses a behavioral question. There may also be instances in which interviewers will not feel the need to ask for a walk-through of your professional history, since it's already visible on your resume. That time can instead be spent more constructively.

What's more, your resume can be the place to highlight specific gains that may not be appropriate for public consumption on LinkedIn. For example:

- If you've done some consulting but your employer or the client companies have a nondisclosure policy or would prefer not to draw attention to it, you might be able to mention such work on a resume or at least MORE specifically than you can on LinkedIn (i.e., "I helped a large retailer based in Bentonville, Arkansas, with a supply-chain-optimization project.").

- You can call out the sizes of budgets or projects that you managed ("I managed a P&L for our sports game division with an annual budget over $20M.").

- You can highlight your impact by citing specific metrics that you've been able to change through your work ("My idea and execution of X directly decreased my firm's expenses by $200K/month.").

Now that you see that having a resume is still relevant, let's explore how to present your resume specific to the PM profession.

Resume Dos

To help you put your best foot forward, here are a few tips and pointers pertaining to what you should include on a resume, proper formatting, and other suggestions.

1. **Do use metrics to quantify your impact whenever possible.** Product managers, and tech leaders generally, are used to thinking in terms of KPIs and success metrics and love to read the percentages by which you increased revenues, retention, DAU, engagement, conversion, etc. If you're coming from a non-Product background, use whatever metrics are most appropriate for your past roles. Discussing how a project you led saved a company large amounts of money is valuable not only because it demonstrates that you paid for yourself but it also shows that you understand the whys behind the work. Product managers must prioritize budgets and keep costs low, so your interviewer will appreciate knowing that you would be mindful of this.

2. **Do convey ownership and an action orientation.** In the descriptions of your current and/or previous professional accomplishments, be specific about what YOU did and contributed. Although giving credit to your teams and colleagues is great, they are not being evaluated in this context. Don't take credit for things you didn't do, but ensure that you're clear about how you performed and what can be traced back to your leadership.

3. **Do highlight your interests.** Many tech jobs don't require cover letters, which are traditionally a mechanism for candidates to communicate some additional color about their experiences, working style, and excitement about potentially joining their target company. There are still opportunities to submit these, but recruiters and hiring managers are spread so thin that they often don't read them (Braxton does!). Tech is generally less traditional than other types of businesses, so it is almost always acceptable to forgo a cover letter and instead include an "Interests" section on your resume. In this section, speak to some of the things that are important to you as a person. Activities such as skiing, surfing, photography, gaming, beekeeping, etc., can make you more memorable or perhaps serve as a way to connect with one or more of your interviewers.

4. **Do feel empowered to send different versions of your resume to different companies.** Recruiters and hiring managers will make their first-tier selections in part by quickly scanning resumes or applications for relevant keywords. Tailoring your submission as closely as possible to

what they are looking for (based on what the job description specified) may help you make that first tier.

Resume Don'ts

1. **Don't directly copy your LinkedIn profile.** Think of your resume as an extension of your LinkedIn profile with additional detail about the very specific things that you've done and how you've made an impact. If you've been a high performer elsewhere, there's a good chance you will be so again at your target company. At least, that's what you want them to think! Having a resume that's identical to your LinkedIn profile comes across as lazy and we wouldn't recommend it. It might not hurt you but it won't help you, and we want you to have every edge over other candidates attempting to land the same job.

2. **Don't include an "objective."** These are pointless fillers and we've never done anything other than read right past them when skimming resumes, usually while feeling mild annoyance. Your objective, from the perspective of the person reading the resume, is that you want to be the person who fills their open role. 'Nuff said.

3. **Don't have any typos or formatting inconsistencies.** There's hardly a more tragic way to screw up your chance of getting a recruiter screen than sloppiness in your grammar, spelling, punctuation, or formatting on your resume. In recent years, the advent of more creative resume formats, especially in tech, has led to a resurgence of these types of issues despite a variety of automated tools to help avoid

them. Give your resume more than a few detailed read throughs before you send it to anyone and get feedback from friends, family, or former colleagues with eyes for detail.

Resume Maybes

1. **Resumes with multiple pages.** There's still some stigma associated with using a resume spanning more than one page, but if anyone uses that as a disqualifier for an otherwise great candidate, we say "OK, Boomer." Many great folks have sufficient work experience—particularly if they started their own companies or had multiple internships starting at an early age—and that relevant information can be difficult to summarize on a single page. That said, there is some argument that it pays to be concise, especially as a PM, and there are certainly ways to trim down. Use your judgment and also ask a few people you trust for their additional perspectives.

2. **Include (very high) standardized test scores.** If you have a near-perfect SAT, GMAT, LSAT, GRE, etc., you may want to think about including it on your resume. One assumption on our side is that you may not want to unduly draw attention to your scores; that said, you should be proud of your performance and these tests (rightly or wrongly) are perceived to be measures of intelligence. Perhaps more importantly, they are evidence of *preparation*, because there are very few people in the world who can walk into an LSAT cold and get a great score. Any such test scores should be found in the "Education" section of your resume.

The Interview Process

Once you've identified some interesting roles and are satisfied with your resume, it's time to start applying. Ideally, you should leverage your contacts for referrals so that you can skip the queue and have a much better chance of moving forward. If you don't know anyone and can't easily get an introduction to someone at your target companies, then it's perfectly fine to apply using LinkedIn or your target companies' websites.

Interview processes can vary wildly from one company to another. Regardless of the company, however, beginning from the time you receive a response to your application, you should expect a multi-week process that entails a series of conversations resembling the following:

- Recruiter screen
- Conversation with hiring manager
- Peer interviews
- Technical/design interview
- Stakeholder interview
- Culture interview
- Conversation with at least one senior leader

We're at step three in our end-to-end description of the entire interview process. Here, we've provided some guidance to help you successfully navigate conversations with recruiters.

Step 3: Acing The Recruiter Screen

After your resume has been perfected and you've applied to your target companies, you'll likely need to pass a recruiter screen as a next step. Regardless of whether you are interviewing with a large company, a semi-mature startup, or a brand new venture, it's common for recruiters with some knowledge of the role to be the first (and ongoing) point of contact for job candidates.

Depending on the circumstances, these might be conducted by internal recruiting staff (almost certainly the case for a large company) or a headhunter who has been contracted to fill specific roles. These screens are sometimes jokingly referred to as "pulse checks" because the first objective is typically to ensure that you are a real, living person who is able to communicate coherently on the phone and that you have product experience relevant to the role. That said, you shouldn't take this conversation for granted and should conduct substantial preparation in advance of the call.

Often, the hiring manager and the recruiter have agreed upon some criteria that the recruiter will be looking for when you tell your story. The recruiter will try to assess the following:

1. Whether the person actually is who she presented herself as on her resume, LinkedIn profile, application, and any email communications before the call

2. If the candidate is a clear communicator and not so nervous or awkward that she would be unable to proceed any further in the interview process (time is a very precious commodity to the hiring manager and other folks that will speak with the candidate in the ensuing rounds)

3. If the candidate is likable and/or a good cultural fit for the company

4. If the candidate is the right fit for the role based on:

- The candidate's understanding and expectations of the role being offered
- The recruiter's perspective for what success will mean
- Seniority, including compensation and any management responsibilities
- Other criteria that may exist, specific to the role

Our general perspective on recruiter screens is that these are a great opportunity for both the company and the candidate to get to know each other at a very high level—to avoid wasting any more of each other's time in the event that it is not a good fit. Think of them as an opportunity for a "first date" before investing any further in the process. If you hear anything that doesn't seem consistent with what you read in the job description or is problematic based on your needs for your next role, you should ask very pointed (yet constructive and polite) questions to help clarify. Don't be afraid to walk away if something doesn't feel right and you aren't encouraged by your discussion with the recruiter on the subject.

In most cases, the recruiter is less likely than a hiring manager or another PM to test you in any particularly rigorous way, with respect to your product management chops. That said, an internal recruiter may have some basic questions designed to assess your fitness for the role. Despite any such stock questions, however, recruiters rarely have personal experience in product management and are not best equipped to evaluate in a detailed way whether you are a product manager in the making or someone who might be better suited for another career path.

Be respectful. Internal recruiters are often, by nature of their personality, well known and liked within their organizations and can torpedo your candidacy if you come across as a jerk. For example, Braxton (as a hiring manager), had one candidate advance from the recruiter screen, but the recruiter conveyed some caveats about perceived rudeness or dismissiveness on that initial call. Although Braxton sensed the potential for a great PM, it was important to him that this person be an enthusiastic team member and a good cultural fit for the organization. In the end, Braxton elected not to interview him. There's not enough time in the day to waste it speaking with assholes!

You, as a candidate, should treat your initial screener as a test subject for how you will sell yourself and your capabilities to the rest of the organization. Be relaxed, gracious, and above all, excited about the opportunity. The last thing you want to do is blow your chance before you are fully through the door.

To prepare for a recruiter screen, we recommend the following:

1. Know your resume inside and out. Practice your "elevator pitch" on friends or family to ensure that you know it cold. Don't sound TOO rehearsed, but be smooth and confident in your delivery.

2. Research your target company thoroughly. Take notes on any major milestones in their history that are publicly available or obtainable from your professional network.

a. When did the company raise its last round of funding or when did it go public?

b. Who are the key leaders?

c. What are the organization's core values?

3. Have a list of questions prepared. You should know what aspects of a new role are most important to you and clarify expectations with the recruiter about what you might expect. For example:

a. Is the role remote or based in an office? Is that office a satellite or the company's headquarters?

b. Who is the hiring manager for the role? (Immediately after the call, go and research this person on LinkedIn and, if you can, speak to anyone in your network who has worked with him or her previously about his or her management style.)

c. What does the product management organization and hierarchy look like? What about UX and visual design? Engineering?

d. Is this a new role or are you replacing someone else? If the latter, how did the role become available? If the person previously in this role was fired, you may have reservations about walking into an unstable organization in which your own job security might be in jeopardy.

e. What tools does the organization use for analytics, A/B testing, and workflow management? The recruiter may not know but is typically impressed by this question, in our experience.

f. What does career progression look like over the longer term? This type of question helps to convey that you are interested in working with the company for a while and are not an opportunistic job hopper.

g. What does success look like in this role? What core skill sets or experience are necessary?

Of course, this is merely a subset of an infinite pool of questions you could ask. We trust that you will create your own list of questions that best speak to what is most important to you, as well as explore the nuances of the opportunity at hand. You should be polite and professional, but don't be afraid to ask the tough questions. We weren't, as we will describe below.

When we were interviewing for Zynga in 2012, the company had recently gone public but the stock had subsequently tanked. There were big questions about the company's ability to sustain growth and revenues, as its viral tactics on Facebook were being severely curtailed by the social networking platform's evolution. Younger, smaller competitors like Supercell (*Hay Day* and *Clash of Clans*) and King (*Candy Crush Saga*) were finding early success on mobile, while Zynga struggled to find its footing in the shifting landscape of casual gaming.

Given the substantial negative press about Zynga at that time, it would have been foolish of us to not acknowledge the reality of the company's struggles. However, we tailored our approach with the recruiter to reflect that we were aware of the issues but still found the opportunity intriguing and compelling. Consequently, we asked questions such as:

1. How is Zynga expediting its transition to mobile given the headwinds it is now facing on the Facebook platform?

2. How is the product management organization developing its talent to innovate in the mobile space?

3. What will Zynga look like in the next two to three years?

Being "real" in your interviews, while simultaneously being constructive and respectful, will almost always serve you well and help you advance. No company is looking for someone who is blindly grasping for a role at any institution that will hire them, regardless of the circumstances—such candidates appear naive and desperate. Better that you demonstrate your understanding of the risks—ask insightful questions about them—and enthusiastically approach the challenges inherent to the role, industry, and company. This attitude is important not only in the recruiter screen, but throughout the entire process.

Step 4: The Take-Home Product Exercise

At some stage during the PM interview process, you may be faced with a Take-Home Exercise. This can occur right after the recruiter screen, or it may be assigned to you later on. Now, before we take a look at the take-home exercise, let's discuss an alternative to it that you might be faced with instead. You should be aware of both of these possibilities, because you could be assigned either one during your own interview process.

Imagine this—you arrive at an unfamiliar office and, after greeting the receptionist and waiting a few minutes in the lobby, you are met by a recruiter and led to a cramped, windowless interview room or booth. After exchanging some pleasantries, the onslaught begins. A parade of PMs, designers, and directors of various development functions cycle through the tiny room, and for each forty-five-minute block, you are subjected to various case questions that test your analytical and structured thinking.

Such questions might include the following:

- Mental or back-of-envelope math, never easy in high-stress situations (nor indicative of real-world job performance). Make a mistake in a funnel calculation and it may be difficult to recover, depending on your interviewer.

- Heavy whiteboarding, including sketching out rough wireframes or user flows. Perhaps the most frustrating for us to see is when the interview team requires the candidate to essentially shorthand an entire feature specification in twenty minutes or less, a task that in the real world might take days or even weeks of substantial iteration before being subjected to a critical eye from any real audience.

- A "brainstorming" session with someone who has substantial institutional knowledge, who may or may not be a willing thought partner, and who also might have their own agenda or preferred candidate who isn't you. Often, there is no formal training or guidance given to these folks. Maybe you give a great first impression and hit on a great idea early in the session, in which case you're golden, but the opposite could just as easily occur.

We spent much of this book trying to help you prepare for these situations and gave you a toolkit to use, in the form of the Compass Framework, to manage them. Even so, for some PM candidates, there is nothing more frightening than the scenarios outlined above. An amazing candidate who has thoroughly prepared and has otherwise great ideas can still encounter pitfalls that easily tank their prospects and take them out of consideration. Isn't there another way? What could be the alternative to this barbaric and grueling interview style?

A modern solution: the take-home product exercise

Thankfully, no-holds-barred interview "firing squads" have largely been replaced with a much more civilized method. The take-home exercise is a homework assignment that is given to candidates who have reached a certain stage of the interview process. This method has become an increasingly popular way to evaluate PM candidates because it allows the candidate a chance to demonstrate core competencies outside of a high-pressure interview environment. As we all know, in-person interviews can be hit or miss based on any number of factors. Many employers have recognized that there is substantial bias inherent to the interview process and have made and are making a concerted effort to try to minimize such bias.

Take-home exercises allow candidates more time to consider and deliberately propose solutions to problems facing the company, while showcasing their PM knowledge and skills. The hiring manager can review the submitted exercise, to ensure that the candidate's work and perspective meet the basic standards of quality, before advancing the candidate. This method further benefits the company because it allows them to take "deeper dives" with more candidates. As an added plus, it is quicker to review take-homes than to engage in a full interview panel.

At the end of the day, the take-home assignment is usually another take on a case question. With that in mind, you can apply the steps of the Compass Framework to help structure your ideas. The Compass Framework principles should help keep your solution appropriately focused and make sure that you hit the important notes throughout your solution. However, we have some additional tips to help you round out your content.

What types of exercises can you expect?

The most common exercises we have observed and heard about from other candidates are those that involve the target company. For example, if interviewing at Uber (who has used take-home exercises for some time), you might be assigned something like the following:

> *What would you consider some of Uber's near-term feature opportunities as well as "big bets?" Articulate a roadmap for the next two quarters.*

In this instance the hiring team most likely expects the candidate to prepare a deck in Microsoft PowerPoint, Google Slides, or Keynote (often the candidate can choose their own format) that will help demonstrate their approach or solutions to the problem. Occasionally, you might get some supplemental material to reference in some way, such as a spreadsheet with data, or some other information that you are expected to include in your answer.

Invest the time

The take-home exercise is a massive opportunity for the candidate to really strut their stuff. Some employers will ask their candidates to timebox their work, typically in a segment of four to six hours. This constraint ensures fairness across all candidates who might be applying for a particular role. After all, some candidates might already have very demanding jobs or other commitments that limit the amount of time that they can spend on an interview assignment. Much like any given role in Product, the work is never really done—most PMs will admit (or gripe) that they could work 24/7 and still have additional things that they could do appropriate to their role: user research, competitive research, data analysis, modeling that supports prioritization of roadmap features . . . and the list goes on.

All that said, if you are given the option, a take-home exercise is one of the best opportunities to differentiate yourself from other candidates. Most employers will NOT impose a time limit, meaning that you can invest as many hours and as much effort as you feel is necessary in order to dazzle the hiring panel. For this reason, we recommend starting the deck as soon as possible after receiving it (perhaps with an outline or some preliminary thoughts and factoids) and then steadily making progress up until the time of submission.

More is more

Conventional wisdom usually dictates that slide content should be kept short, to avoid distracting your audience. We suggest taking this advice with a grain of salt. More often than not, you'll be asked to submit your deck in advance of delivering it live, so that the hiring panel can preview it. If this happens, your planned voiceover will be irrelevant as you won't be able to fully explain your ideas until you are there in person (or on Zoom)—and by then, first impressions will already have been cast.

In order to please the hiring panel when they preview your deck, as well as leave something to dazzle them with when you deliver your presentation live, you'll want to find the right balance between slides that are too wordy and those one-word slides that strive to make the mic-drop impacts at a TED Talk.

While impact is essential, so is clarity. A variety of slide formats that can be clearly followed whether or not you are delivering the accompanying narrative, will keep your previewers interested and lead them to want to hear the full presentation from you. Use tables or charts to organize metrics that would be important to your prospective employers. Make a diagram displaying the core loop of the product (labeled, of course). A compelling assignment will probably include dozens but not hundreds of slides, if that is the format they prescribed.

We would also recommend going beyond the scope of the task. For example, you might be asked to identify a number of features that would make sense for your prospective employer's product and indicate how you would prioritize them. The bare minimum here might be two slides—the first with your proposed features and the second with a sequenced list. However, don't let it escape you that the true, underlying purpose of the exercise is actually to evaluate how you think *and* the methodologies that you would bring to the organization. With that in mind, a better approach for your deck structure might be:

- Inputs for feature ideas: product metrics, ideas from teams, customer feedback, competitors

- A section with features, including some wireframes and **t-shirt costing** as well as estimated upsides based on the metrics you'd like to move

- Methodology for prioritization: RICE or other frameworks (see Chapter 5)

- A timeline showing your sequence of features, perhaps across multiple teams or squads, and indicating any **dependencies**

- Any trade-offs that you might incur given the sequencing that you've chosen

- Your product development process (e.g., research, design exploration, one-pager, full specification, development, QA, A/B testing, analysis, iteration)

Q&A

Most interview panels will also expect you to leave time at the end of your presentation to answer a few questions (although they may also have peppered them into your presentation). Given an hour to present, you may want to plan for, and practice, about forty-five minutes of content so that time will be available for questions and additional discussion.

There is a natural tendency to speed up one's delivery when presenting in front of a live audience, sometimes driven by nervousness, which is one of the reasons that running through your case solution a few times in advance of the live delivery is important. Additionally, you will almost inevitably lose some time during your presentation as you take questions, clarify comments, or field other tangents from the interview panel. Thus, it's good to leave yourself some buffer.

Step 5: Onsite

During the onsite phase, you will most likely have a large number of interviews with various people at the company or on the team during a single day. Here, your knowledge of the Compass Framework and the different types of PM case questions will come into play. If you feel the need, go back to the chapters that covered those topics and reacquaint yourself with them. Below are some additional logistical notes about what to expect onsite.

The onsite is one of our favorite aspects of the interview process. If you've made it this far, things have generally gone well for you and you should be excited about the prospect of receiving an offer if you can continue to impress the hiring panel.

Like any other part of the process, the onsite is an opportunity for you to learn more about the company and the team, and it is also a major part of their evaluation of you. It's important that you maintain high energy and a positive attitude from the moment you walk into the building.

Some of this may sound obvious, but you should do whatever it takes to ensure that you have a full night's sleep beforehand; as well, take the time to look your best, get your morning coffee, and do whatever else is necessary for you to be your best self.

At least some of the folks with whom you'll speak during an onsite will be evaluating you primarily for culture fit rather than for technical skills. Especially if you've already completed a take-home assignment or some case interviews, the additional interviews during an onsite are more likely intended to assess how you would fit into the team, whether you would be a good partner to other key folks within the organization, and perhaps how you exemplify the organization's core values. If such values exist and are publicly available (or were provided to you), you should think about and write down in advance some professional examples of how you've embraced those values.

A quick note on dress code: tech companies are generally casual environments. You might receive some guidance on what is appropriate but it's usually a good idea to dress just slightly more formally than those with whom you're speaking that day. For both women and men, it might make sense to wear a blazer (but never a suit!).

Visiting a company is a rare chance to think about whether a role is a good fit for *you*. Consider:

- Were you given an office tour? How did you like the building or campus and is it somewhere you could see yourself working?

- Did the employees seem happy?

- Did you like the final set of interviewers? Did they seem like people with whom you would enjoy working?

- Was the onsite process professionally planned and executed?

You're almost there! Keep your cool, power through the onsite and you should have a good chance of receiving an offer.

Step 6: What Happens Next?

The stars align

After the onsite, the bulk of your work is done. Ideally, you've been a strong candidate and you've persuaded the hiring manager to invite you to join the team. Immediately after concluding the process or perhaps within a few days, you're told that you'll be receiving an offer. Congratulations!

This is a great place to be and even better if you have offers from multiple companies. If you haven't already, you should use this time to ask any remaining hard questions about the opportunities at hand and assess whether any of them is the right fit for you. You may want to write out pros and cons of making a change, for example. It would also be a good idea to see if you have anyone in your network who has also worked, or works, at the company, who might be able to shed some good insight in an unbiased way.

Assuming you remain genuinely interested in the opportunities you have garnered, you should also try to negotiate the terms of your offers. We have not encountered any better high-density guidance for this situation than that offered in two blog posts by Haseeb Qureshi ("Ten Rules for Negotiating a Job Offer" and "How Not to Bomb Your Offer Negotiation"). Among all the helpful tips he presents to his readers, one particularly stands out: be winnable. You should remain positive, outline clear steps for the company on what it would take for you to sign, and articulate clear reasons for any additional requests to amend their initial offer (from salary or paid time off, to your title).

In any event, this is a time to acknowledge what you've accomplished and look forward to what will hopefully be an exciting new step in your career!

When it's not a fit

Imagine that a friend or former colleague referred you to what seems like your dream company or role, and so far you've done everything right. You nailed the recruiter screen, had a great call with the hiring manager, utilized the Compass Framework and competently answered your case questions with various members of the Product team, and you completed a take-home exercise and presented it to the hiring panel. You're feeling confident. A few days later, you get a call from your recruiter:

- "We've decided to go in another direction."

- "Another candidate has more relevant experience."

- "The team felt that your approach may not be quantitative enough for our culture."

Ouch. It really stings to be turned down. You had your heart set on this opportunity and, for whatever reason, it didn't work out.

As we've alluded to and directly discussed many times throughout *Product Sense*, product management can vary drastically from one company to the next. Different organizations and products may have very different needs when trying to fill a role. There could be many reasons why a particular opportunity doesn't work out but, if the hiring team decides you aren't the right fit and does not give you an offer, try not to let it get you down.

We, the authors, are no strangers to rejection in our own professional careers. Let's walk through how we have approached it so that you'll be better prepared when things don't go your way.

Preparing yourself for rejection

First of all, you should know that almost everyone, no matter how intelligent, well connected, or prepared they are, will face rejection at some point. The reality is that no one is a fit for every job out there. Even if you *believe* you are the perfect candidate for a position, there may be criteria that you're not aware of that the recruiting team and hiring manager are dealing with behind the scenes. Another, more suitable candidate could come along or there might be an internal transfer who has company knowledge that you, as an outsider, simply don't possess.

From our perspective, you should go into every interview process with low expectations and assume that you will not get the position. Don't celebrate until your offer is in hand! This mindset will serve you for two reasons:

1. If you are rejected, you will not be as crushed when you get the bad news.

2. You will not take anything for granted during the process and will put your best effort into researching the company and opportunity, practicing cases, completing the take-home exercise, and doing anything else required.

Granted, there is a possible downside to this approach—assuming that you will not get the job may dampen any excitement you feel about it. So you have to find the balance between bringing a high level of enthusiasm to the interviews and not becoming too emotionally invested. It's a very fine line to walk and we aren't always able to do it, either, but adopting this mindset will allow you to view the interview process as a chance to perfect your interviewing skills.

When you're rejected

First, ask for feedback! The worst they can say is no. Many companies will be happy to share feedback about why you weren't selected for a particular position. If that information isn't volunteered, it should be one of the first things you ask as you close out the process with them:

"I'm very disappointed to hear that. Thank you for your time and consideration. Is there any information you could share about why the team decided not to proceed with my candidacy? I'd love to know where I can improve or how I can be a stronger applicant in the future."

At this point, especially if you've had a few calls or done an onsite with the company, many recruiters will share whatever reasons they can about why you didn't get the job.

If not, you may be able to draw some conclusions on your own. Think about the following:

- Were there any interviews that you felt didn't go well? If so, why, and how can you avoid a similar situation in the future?

- How was your performance on the case questions or take-home exercise that you completed, if applicable? Would you do anything differently if you saw the same case/exercise again?

- Were there any recurring themes or questions during your interviews? You might be able to hone in on a potential area of weakness or concern if multiple people asked you the same question.

What to do next

Let's say you received some feedback about why you weren't selected or were able to identify some potential areas of improvement on your own. What should you do next? Here are a couple of examples from the authors:

Sometimes it just isn't the right fit (Braxton)

During my job search in the summer of 2020 (during the pandemic), the competition was especially fierce. Those companies that *were* hiring had many great candidates from which to choose. One company I spoke with in the pet-care space was looking for a Head of Product. After speaking to the hiring manager on the executive team, as well as a product manager, I felt the process was going well. My next call was with the Director of Engineering, who asked me a number of fairly technical questions (relative to most PM interview loops I've encountered). After this call, I was rejected. I immediately asked for feedback and was told that the team was looking for someone more technical. In this case, I didn't take any specific action because I didn't think that the effort required to become a *much* more technical PM would be worthwhile for me at my level of seniority; in other words, it was just bad luck on my part that I either a) didn't come across as technical enough or b) this particular role simply wasn't a fit for me, given my non-technical background and that team's requirements. It's never a bad idea to become more technical but I didn't take any corrective action afterward, in this case.

Tuning the take-home for an audience (Peter)

I was looking for a new role and was in the final rounds for a Lead PM position, which would also serve to be the first PM hired at this small company. Things were going along well, albeit rushed since I came in late in the process. I presented my take-home . . . to almost the entire staff of seventeen folks! This was especially challenging because, in many instances, a successful hire needs pretty much unanimous support from the deliberating team. So it raised my chances of failure since there were just more people involved in the process. Regretfully, I did not get the job, and the CEO messaged me with the feedback that one or two people were unclear about some of the concepts I was trying to articulate. In hindsight I think the lesson for me was to be aware of the audience, know who was going to be in the meeting and tailor the content to make sure it will be clear to all.

As you may discern from these examples, you might gain (through feedback or reflection) a sense of where you can improve. Pick yourself up and accept the momentary setback as an opportunity for improvement: this particular job didn't work out, but you can use the feedback to help you become a stronger candidate in the future. After all, these very situations are reflective of how products are built in the world of a PM—we use data and customer feedback to iterate something better.

Another possibility to keep in mind is that, perhaps, the job you didn't get wasn't the right fit for you. An initial question we like to ask when speaking with a recruiter or hiring manager is what the "Product philosophy" of the company is; in other words, how the company views the role and responsibilities of a PM. Depending on your background or interests, you may have certain criteria that you are trying to meet and, if a company or role isn't the right fit, you should feel OK about walking away or being deemed as a mismatch. As Braxton noted in his first example, in which the hiring team determined that he was "not technical enough," despite his extensive Product experience and skills, that company/role probably wouldn't have worked out. It was far better to learn this during the interview process than after investing substantial time and effort to acclimate into a new role in a context that might ultimately result in disappointment for everyone involved. Product managers are not a commodity, and the best fit can be harder to achieve than you think. These things happen and are the nature of the game.

Conclusion

It has been our honor to share this journey with you! By now, you have come a long way in your preparation for a job in product management. You should feel as proud of yourself as we are of you, and also much more confident in your quest to land your dream role. Before we "sign off," let's step back and reflect on what we have covered in this book.

We began *Product Sense* by discussing, well, the concept of product sense. Through our explanations and demonstrations, we showed you that product sense is a key awareness that every PM needs to cultivate in order to be successful on the job, and every PM candidate needs to demonstrate during the interview process. *As we emphasized throughout the book, product sense is a skill that can be learned.* With careful practice, one can master the art of thinking about products and the users who buy them, and how to identify and solve user pain points. It *is* possible to adopt the mindset of product sense. Make no mistake, it is absolutely possible to show your interviewers that you are the diamond in the rough that they are seeking—the candidate with the potential to grow a great capacity for product sense—the one who will masterfully orchestrate product management and be an asset to their organization.

In Part 1, we discussed the fundamental question that every PM confronts and seeks to answer on a daily basis, "What should we build and why?" A skillful PM is always thinking about this question, communicating with stakeholders and customers about it, and structuring their roadmaps based on how it might be answered. We also looked at several other key skills and activities in the PM role: demonstrating user empathy, identifying pain points, using metrics to inform product thinking and decision-making, establishing a product vision, and finding that ever-important North Star Metric. This portion of the book also gave you insight into how PMs view the world, a clearer idea of the kinds of conversations you will likely encounter in your interviews, and solid strategies to help you frame your answers to those key questions.

Next came Part 2, in which we uncovered the four major types of Product case questions: Product Sense and Design, Execution, Product Strategy, and Leadership. We walked you through some examples of these questions as well as sample answers. We provided these examples as a starting point, but there are many sample questions that can be found online. As you prepare for the interview process, answering these practice questions—while applying the techniques we have outlined for you, ideally with a friend or mentor—will be essential preparation as you flex your PM muscles in pursuit of your first PM role.

Our Compass Framework, as you now know, is an approach you can use to answer case questions in a structured way. Keep in mind that, while the framework is a useful tool that will help you touch on all the critical points that interviewers will look for in your responses, what's most important is that you can answer questions both methodically and succinctly. Your interviewer will need to understand your reasoning and perceive that you would be a good thought partner if you were to join the team.

This is why we crafted the Compass Framework to be very flexible to your needs "in the moment" while you are in a conversation with an interviewer. Following the framework and applying it to your answer, step by step, will keep you focused without sounding rigid or rehearsed. That is the beauty of this framework over the others we have encountered in our careers. The Compass Framework will help you to show *how* you are arriving at a solution for your case question—which will in turn show your interviewer that you have the thinking skills, patience, mindset, and tenacity to solve real problems on the job.

In Part 3, we discussed the job-hunting process, including some of the different paths that might lead to a PM job (internships, internal transfers, rotational programs, etc.). We looked at how to choose a target company based on your preferences and fit, how to separate yourself from the crowd, and the different types of interview processes that you're likely to encounter. We also shared our thoughts on how to approach the pivotal "take-home exercises" that have become popular in recent years, and even how to deal with rejection.

So what now?

There's no two ways about it, getting a PM job is *hard*. We know and we can relate. On the career-finding front, we have experienced both euphoric successes and soul-crushing failures. Additionally, we have spent countless hours discussing the PM recruiting process with numerous others who have been through it: as coaches, mentors, and friends.

We wanted to write this book because this discipline can be such a black box to those living outside of it. Our hope is that, through all that we have shared in this book, we will not only make getting that PM job easier for you, but that we have already demystified what life on the job might look like. In part, we believe that providing a perspective on the PM "lifestyle" will help those who are curious decide whether they really want to take the leap into Product, and give those natural but undiscovered PMs the push they need to step into the role they were born for.

To that end, we've included the transcripts of interviews with several PM leaders as supplemental material following this section. We were delighted to connect with other PM leaders who have important perspectives on how the profession has matured over the last ten years and to discuss and debate what a PM is and what it takes to excel in the field. On top of serving as background research for *Product Sense,* conducting these interviews turned out to be an important part of our personal journey. The experience helped us to see our own roles and the challenges we have faced (and still face) from new and different angles. For those interested in some of the companies where these folks have worked, we hope that these interviews will be as enjoyable as they are insightful.

After the PM interview transcripts, you'll find a glossary of many of the PM terms used in this book and in the PM role. Jargon/terminology/lingo/shoptalk, whatever you want to call it, in relation to a specific industry or professional position, can be difficult to master before one is "on the inside." Our hope is that defining some common PM terms and phrases will help to expand your understanding and mindset of the role before you have that first conversation with a recruiter. We hope to give you an edge!

If you do decide to take the plunge and become a PM, know that we will be right there with you. As you follow your PM path, we hope that you will return to this resource again and again—as a source of preparation as well as inspiration. If we may leave you with one sentiment, it's that being a PM requires passion (and we hope we have sparked that passion in *YOU)*. Product management can be lucrative, exciting, and rife with opportunities for you to demonstrate leadership and analytical thinking. However, it can also set before you obstacle after obstacle and is sometimes (often?) thankless. You may find yourself in the office creating PRDs long after the rest of your team has gone home for the night, or at the center of complex and emotion-fueled intercompany disputes.

Despite these challenges, being a PM is an incredible opportunity for those with a strong growth mindset to have an enormous impact on users and customers, and to potentially make the world a better place. Your work will create enhanced product experiences that strengthen your business as you employ a more thoughtful approach to introducing new products to the masses.

When we began our first PM jobs nearly a decade ago, we had no idea that we would still be in Product all these years later. For us, it *did* become a calling, and we found our passion for it despite the many ups and downs that we've had in our careers.

We're excited for you to embark on your PM journey! The product community is an intimate niche and we'd love for you to be part of it. Good luck and good hunting.

—Peter and Braxton

PART 4

PM Leader Interviews

Throughout *Product Sense,* we have incorporated the thoughts, lessons, and collective wisdom of dozens of product managers—all interviewed as background research for this book. Here, we've included selected transcripts from a few of those folks, in order to give you an inside look into the world of product management.

These individuals have grown their careers in Product and simultaneously helped to sculpt what Product is in the tech industry. From their first PM roles, into more senior positions, and eventually to leadership roles on their teams, each has forged a path that newer PMs should want to emulate and follow. In addition to their professional histories, we asked them to describe their hiring philosophies, and what they look for when evaluating candidates.

Each person experiences and perceives the PM role differently, and we hope that you will glean useful and additional perspective as you read each interview.

Kevin Sung

Director of Product Management at Dropbox

What does product management mean to you?

Kevin: I have had three product management roles at three different companies, and product management has meant very different things at each of the companies. At Zynga, product management was the lifeblood of the games—trying to figure out business results for each game that was being made, [and] balancing out the creative folks. At Smule, Product was more like a facilitator between engineering and project management, and trying to keep things on schedule. At Dropbox, teams work fairly autonomously. So product managers are, I feel, more like strategic planners trying to achieve cross-team alignment across the company. The product manager, to me, is the person who is responsible for the results and also the glue that holds a project together.

The joke is that the product manager gets blamed if anything goes wrong, but when things go right, the team is praised. The job is to keep something together and you're graded on the results.

Kevin: A more senior colleague told me that he felt that it was his job to be blamed. You are literally hired, especially as you reach director and VP levels, to shield the team from fear and uncertainty so that they feel empowered to go and do the right things for the customer. Then your job is to be blamed if things go wrong, and you hope that in that period of time between the blame and when you started, that some good things were done.

You said something interesting about being a facilitator. How would you see the role of product manager changing as someone progresses from being an associate PM—fresh out of college—up to, say, the director level? How does that arc of responsibilities change?

Kevin: To me, it's the scope and independence [that] increases as you grow in tenure. As an associate, you are focused on execution of ideas that may not be your own, but have been thought of by other people. It's really about whether you can build on an idea already at a one or two, rather than from zero to one. As you ramp up and grow your career, when you become a more senior product manager—eventually a director—your scope changes. Beyond just the project, you now own an area or a more complex problem. You are thinking of different projects all at once, and beyond just simply the delivery of a feature. At the director or VP level, you're in charge of strategic direction and business outcomes that span across multiple parts of a larger company.

It depends on the company, too. There are companies that are very product driven, where Product is able to define strategy. There are other companies where tech meets commerce, in which, maybe, it's marketing that actually calls the shots and product managers are really there to work with engineering. So, I'm really speaking of a Product-led type of tech company.

Who drives the strategy? How does that happen?

Kevin: To me, ownership is very important. That means the person who drives the strategy is the person who is responsible for the results. So, the worst thing you want to do is be in a situation where a product manager is blamed for something he or she had zero control over. If you're going to make someone responsible for the results, you need to give them the autonomy to go and figure out what the game board looks like, where and who the pieces are, what game we're playing, what the rules are, and what moves we need to make. That doesn't always happen. Sometimes you have smaller companies run by a strong-willed CEO who's really more like a product thinker who kind of dictates things. We have a very large company where Sales has different ideas and products.

In general, my philosophy is that if you're responsible for the results, you need to have autonomy. At Dropbox, the leadership executives will set a North-Star type of metric that you might look at for the next year, or the next three years, and then middle management—director-level product managers who have an area of ownership—set sub metrics. However, they give the more junior product managers the ability to come up with their own features. But you might need to work with Marketing, who says "Hey, we have an event in October and we need to work backwards from that. What are the features that will be ready?" The product manager may have ideas but also timeline challenges. Ideally you have full autonomy over your roadmap, but it often doesn't work out that way.

What do you find most challenging about working in Product?

Kevin: It depends on your company. My current company is very, very large and so the alignment and incentives between different product managers and teams can be challenging. Occasionally, goals become misaligned, and there are two different ways to deal with that. Some product managers will do an "us-versus-you" type of thing. We're going to grind, go after the numbers, and we will win. Some PMs will try to work together to surface up different ways in which the organization can align metrics so that everyone is swimming in the same direction.

That's something that comes with maturity, and also a willingness by the company and by middle management to actually listen and make changes. Suppose executives at a company establish a WAU or MAU goal that everyone needs to hit; for example, three times that number in three years. And Team X thinks, "Okay, well, we're going to have an MAU-A," and then Team Y says, "We're going to have an MAU-B." But those two teams are fighting for, or creating features, for the same surface area.

There may be a big question about who gets credit for the MAU. And it might speak to a problem in leadership—that they did not define well enough how to split credit between two different teams, so that they can effectively work together. The biggest challenge in dealing with situations like that, to get others to work with you, is through incentives. I'd say a lot of my job is actually building relationships, and trying to realign incentives, so that my team is able to execute on projects. Executives may not always know the details on the ground.

It's often good to give other teams credit because that actually allows the teams to work together and build.

So if you were to coach a junior PM, how would you tell him or her to navigate that? How can you advise them to split the credit when you have two people competing over one metric?

Kevin: Firstly, you have to manage up. You have to manage your own manager because your manager is being told to go after MAU at any cost. So you have to push back and say, "Actually, we shouldn't go after this alone for these reasons." Once the manager's on your side, you go convince the other side, and then you have to convince whoever's in charge of the mechanism in which these metrics are then rolled upwards—because a lot of people miss that the danger that companies fall into, is that they just look at a number and they try to move it. They don't really understand the meaning behind the number, or that the number is meant to guide you, so that when you're in an ambiguous situation you have a North Star.

Another thing to consider: sometimes the integrity of the data that you're looking at is suspect. A/B testing is a great tool if you know what you're doing with it (for a specific purpose), but people sometimes rely on A/B testing a little too much for all of their decision making, and they are blind to the flaws of the process.

We all started in a place where A/B testing was very common; but at that time there wasn't much other user research happening. As your Product career has progressed, have you done more things like surveys, prototyping, and user observation, or user interviews?

Kevin: So, talking to users is very important. We have a strong user-research function here, and we run a program called "Real-World Wednesdays" where we bring in five to ten folks off the street, or recruited from a Product area's channels. No matter what team you're on, you can sign up and run examples or mock-ups by them—

talk to them, have them walk through prototypes that you've built—and just sit back and observe. I've found that to be very, very helpful.

Early in my career, I held a flawed perspective that, "You don't need to talk to users, because the big data will tell you everything," and I didn't want to over-index on one user, because that one user may not know what they're talking about. I now have a more moderate mindset that I should still use the data, but that the data doesn't tell you everything, and that the qualitative can help explain the quantitative—both exist, simultaneously.

You may even want to start with qualitative first, because it can inform or help shape your hypothesis about the user problem you're trying to solve, which will eventually affect adoption of your feature. It needs to be validated from the beginning before you even start instrumenting any kind of analytics, because if your hypothesis about that problem is wrong, your work won't matter. So, talk to five or ten real users and if they give you directionally positive feedback—even though it's probably not perfect—you've gained a valuable signal that you're on the right track. If a few of them think you're missing the mark, then you may have just avoided six months of a very costly investment.

You should still track product usage, of course. There's this phenomenon I've seen where a lot of companies don't like to talk to users and really focus on the data. They rely on intuition but without the early validation, and they build something and they release it—after which adoption is kind of slow. Then, they put a Growth team on it to juice the numbers by fixing the onboarding, or making some questions appear in a modal that will drive the users to a feature so that they're aware of it. Then they end up annoying their users by pushing them to something that the users don't really care about. That could be avoided if, from the beginning, you were validating the user problem that you were solving.

I've also recently "seen the light" about qualitative research, and I think it's a result of being in the B2B space, because I'm not working on a consumer product with a million data points every day. How many data points is one hour of user research worth? It's probably worth a lot.

Kevin: Possibly. It depends on the customer that you're talking to. There's also a pitfall to that approach: if you don't have an idea of what to do, a customer is never going to tell you exactly what he wants. I still believe that you don't want to over-index on just one person's opinion, but I think it's a combination. You should have an initial hypothesis about what the user's problem is, but go and validate whether the hypothesis is correct or not by talking to real users. There's always a risk that you'll speak with an outlier user who gives you contrary information.

To me, though, everything's risk management and it's better to deepen your understanding of the problem rather than not talk to users at all. Every company should talk to users in some way. Can't get them in person? Do a survey. Can't do a survey? Talk to colleagues who don't use the product, or friends or family, or run through a flow yourself. They're all different degrees of effectiveness but you need to do something.

One point on the value of the user is: if you're in the B2B enterprise space, you probably have a small handful of huge companies that make up the vast majority of your revenue. At each one, there's probably an IT admin who is running the show and has a strong opinion about what things you need to build. That's a case where you should talk to *that* customer and they'll tell you exactly what they need in order for you to land a deal. A totally different beast, but it still falls under the same umbrella. Customer support is actually a great source for insights, as well, since they are speaking with the customers all the time and can often identify themes or complaints that can inform your roadmap.

I think that some customer-support agents probably understand the products better than the product managers themselves. Often, they have a wide view of the entire product (how it works, and all [of] its problems), unlike a product manager who might be laser focused in a single area. A customer-support agent that wants to transition to Product already has a strong foundation and just needs to build on it.

I know a few people who have gone from Customer Support to Product. It took three or four years and these are very high-quality folks.

Kevin: That's where smaller companies are beneficial. If you're in a large company, you're stuck in the bureaucracy and you can't change roles. A lot of people go to a smaller company where they just need people and you can get your Product chops, and then later go back to a big company, if you want.

It can be pretty ridiculous when (at a big company), they say, "I want ten years of Product experience." Uh, do you want someone from HP? The person will have no mobile background. I don't know if you're an executive at that level. I think sometimes people are a little too strict on the numbers in the job description document. Anyone who has traditional PM experience right now might have a maximum of ten or twelve years—not that much. Most of them probably started at Amazon, Zynga, or Google.

How do you think about past experience when you're evaluating PM candidates?

Kevin: It's varied. In the past, I might have needed someone who knew what vendors to talk to, who could come in and hit the ground running because I'm working in a hire-fast/fire-fast culture. Dropbox is different. There is a lot more structure and a very high bar for core skills, leveling, and scope. But there is also a strong support and mentorship system in place to set individuals up for success.

On top of that, I personally look for individuals that spike on ownership, and ability to deal with complexity and ambiguity, and learn meaningful lessons from their failures.

Dropbox has a very structured hiring process for product managers, where we determine if you're a good fit for Dropbox separately from if you're a good fit for the specific team or role you're interviewing for. The process is fair and highly optimized, as we want to be able to compare apples to apples. Hiring managers make the ultimate decision, but are able to gather strong signals from a variety of methods, and have faith that it's rigorous and equitable.

However, there are so many books out there that prepare people for interviews, that I sometimes wonder if interviewing ultimately evaluates a candidate's study habits and ability to parrot talking points, rather than product sense, skill, and judgment. Ultimately, it's important to continually evaluate your interview process, compare to industry peers, and keep calibrating to the right signal.

Khalid Ashour

Staff Product Manager at Twitter, Former Product Manager at Facebook

Khalid, what does product management mean to you?

Khalid: Rarely do you find a clear definition, which ends up being really more confusing for people who want to move into the field. There aren't many resources by which you can learn and you don't go to school for it. After working for eight years or so in this space, my perspective is that the job exists to figure out what we should be building.

It doesn't necessarily have to be in a visionary sense, "This is my vision, from my ivory tower." It could be very collaborative. It depends on the context and the company and who you are as a person. Everything you do on a daily basis—roadmapping meetings, cross-functional collaboration, anything—it's really serving that purpose because you're the multiplier on awesomeness. Your team can probably do things without a PM: they have engineers who can code, the designer can design, but the end result is not going to be larger than the sum of its parts, so to speak.

That's where the PM comes in. That's the core value of the role. Sometimes a PM thinks, "Oh, I should be coding or designing." It's cool if you want to do those [things] if you just have a preexisting skill set; but at the same time, if I do any code, I'm probably going to mess up things for the engineers because it's not my core value. I would focus on my value as a PM, which is, "What should we build and why?"

What do you think distinguishes a good PM or an excellent PM from a bad PM?

Khalid: Generally, the behaviors, attitudes, and aptitudes that I've found from my own experience—and also [from] seeing other PMs operate—that make an effective PM, are communication skills.

Communication is important because, in any situation where you're leading a team, everyone has to be at least moving in the right direction and be clear about what they should be doing. Communication and messaging are the vehicles to do that. Also, there are PMs who are able to extract information from everyone around them and involve everyone. You don't have to make a consensus decision, but you should explore everyone's point of view. If you can see the problem from as many angles as you can, you will probably get to a better end decision.

Customer empathy or familiarity is key. You are building a product to solve a user problem. If you're not familiar with the user—thinking, "Who are they? In what contexts do they have this problem, and in what context would they use the products, and what are their values?" or, "Are they price sensitive? Are they time sensitive?" all these things—you will find it more difficult to understand what problems they might have and then come to a solution, which again, goes back to, "What should we build and why?"

What do you find are the most challenging aspects of working in Product?

Khalid: Here are a few things that come to mind, one is ambiguity. Consider a spectrum of "very objective" to "very subjective." On the objective end, two plus two equals four—it's a fact. There's a world of facts. On the other end, there's the whole other extreme world in which, if I were to recommend the best vacation to my friends, for example, there's no objectively correct answer. For Pete, it might be on a beach somewhere, but for Braxton, it's a skiing destination. Even if it's a beach, what kind of beach? Is it quiet or is it full of people? This is more of just a normal decision that you'd make in your day-to-day life. But I think that the analog to Product is that there are problems and decisions that are very ambiguous when you, as a PM, are solving something.

Maybe your solution makes the experience good for some people but not as good for others. To what *degree* it creates a good experience for some people versus worse for others may not have a straightforward answer. For example, if I consider Lyft or Uber, you have a supply (which is the network of drivers), and you have demand (represented by the riders), and you're matching these two in some way. There are situations where you have to trade off, such as, "Do I make the experience more favorable for the rider at the expense of the driver, or vice versa?" How do you make these decisions? Is it a value judgment, or do you build mechanisms, or is it arbitrary? I think ambiguity is probably one of the more challenging things.

Secondly, and this differs between smaller or bigger companies, but stakeholder management can be challenging. Even when you do have all the answers, which isn't often [the] reality, you might find yourself in a situation where you have to get a number of executive-level stakeholders to reconcile disagreements. You have to sort this out because you can't effectively move forward without resolution or alignment. Sometimes, again, those conversations are not necessarily based on facts or data. Some stakeholders might be *moved* by data, but some won't change their position, because maybe they're incentivized to do something else or your solution is in conflict with their goals.

The last challenge—and this is a really important one—[is] if you ask a fish, "What is it like underwater?", the fish won't answer, "It's wet!", because the fish takes that condition for granted. That is such a simple dynamic with PM'ing when it comes to your individual career, always be conscious of where you objectively stand within your organization.

Sometimes, the attribution of PM value is very difficult. With an engineer, it's pretty objective. I can see how many lines of code they're writing. I can understand what their code is doing, and so on. For a designer, I can see the quality of their designs and assess whether people like them, as well as the timeline on which they're delivering. With a product manager, you can't A/B test two universes and see how the team would perform with a PM versus without one. Sometimes you'll find your value questioned by many different people or perhaps you'll even question yourself, "How am I doing with the team?" Sometimes that link between your own work as a PM and [the] final results is not very clear, and can affect your personal motivation; it affects perception and basically all sides of the equation.

How do you measure the value of the individual PM?

Khalid: That's what I was trying to express with the fish-in-the-water metaphor—and why I think it's helpful as a PM or a potential PM to understand this aspect of the job—because for my first two or three years as a PM, I couldn't even clearly articulate my own value. There was this background feeling of dissonance, "Am I doing what I should be doing? Is this really the job or not?" Understanding that this is part of the job helps you deal with it and accept it.

Do you have any good examples where you observed conflicting stakeholder expectations or objectives? How did you, or the person that you saw in this situation, handle that?

Khalid: I'll try to paint a generic situation. Usually, there's a couple of things. One is off the get go, there's the question of, "Do you have the wrong setup, or do you have the wrong expectations?" The second part is, "With what you have, how can you align all points of view?"

What I mean by "having the right setup" is that you try to surface or unpack all useful information, but as a PM or a product team, there's no way you can optimize and solve for a thousand different points of view. You may inherently have to answer to twenty different people, which may be a broken setup and is not realistically possible.

Off the top, you have to find a way—either through your own work, or through getting support [from] your manager and maybe other leadership—to set the right expectation and define who the stakeholders that matter are, and what we're solving.

There are situations I've been in where circumstances were such that it was difficult to move forward, and there are situations in which it was much easier to do so. The difference I have found is, you have to have some respected, very senior person to whom everyone can defer, "So what does the escalation path look like?" Because at our level, if our goals are just inherently different, we need one step up to be able to make a trade-off and say, "What is more important for the company?" In that sense, the job we're doing is to provide them with the facts and the information as much as possible, so that they can facilitate a group decision.

Short of an escalation path, sometimes you can start to work things along with a group. You think long term about, "How can we de-risk the situation as much as possible? If we make this trade-off, it's going to hurt you in this way. If we make the other, it will hurt the other team in that way. Is there a way we can attain the maximum benefit but without much of the cost to the other team?" Or, can you make an argument to show that maybe this is slightly detrimental in the short term, but over the long term, there's value that justifies the decision?

The last bit, maybe the easiest one to mitigate, is that sometimes we're just working off different data and pieces of information. Make sure that everyone sees the same picture. If I have an insight that making a change would drive this much incremental revenue and you don't, you will come to different conclusions. I think your responsibility as a PM is to be factual or objective in these situations, to be a truth seeker and to be proactive about involving the people who need to be involved.

When you're hiring a product manager, what traits do you look for?

Khalid: There are core skills that generally people tend to value and try to focus on, things like structured thinking, communication, analytical ability and inclination, user empathy, etc. I think I tend to over-index on self-awareness—which you can get a sense of from how the person is talking—and also attitude, more so than the aptitude skills, because I think all of the other things you can teach but it's harder or sometimes impossible to teach the right attitude.

By "right attitude," I mean things such as treating the product like it's your own business, being an owner, and not expecting to be told what you should do. Being open to feedback and working together with people. There's certainly a base level for PM skills, but assuming that's there, then the differentiator is really the attitude.

As you're trying to identify whether a candidate has the right attitude, what types of questions do you ask the candidates that you speak to?

Khalid: I might ask them, "How might some specific part of a product work?" Or let's say there's an area that they're an expert in and I'm not and I ask them about it. If their tone during the conversation is, "Oh, don't worry about that," (maybe not verbatim but their answer is somehow problematic in tone) then I might see that this is not going to be the right person. If they take the time to explain to you and so on, it tells me two things: that they understand what they're talking about rather than just making sh** up, and that they can communicate and help the other person to also understand what they're talking about.

Sometimes, as far as questions go, let's say we start with a prompt such as, "How might you solve . . . " or, "Oh, build Lyft for kids, how might you do that?" There's generally a process that you as a candidate will follow to identify the right solution to build. Don't jump into a solution immediately: define the problem, define the users, and so on, and that's all good. Again, you'd hope that's what they're doing, but at the same time, if they don't do that and they make a mistake such as jumping directly into a solution, I try to nudge them and guide them a bit. If they course correct, it's okay. I would say that's fine. They responded to feedback. If they keep going in that same direction rather than taking that feedback, I think that's a negative sign.

How do you see interviewing for PMs having changed over the last five years?

Khalid: There's much more information these days about what types of questions are asked. Sometimes, companies or people worry about their questions coming out such that people will start gaming them. Although there is more information and knowledge on what to expect, I think you can still tell who's a good candidate or not because, even if the questions are on the internet, a good interviewer will always throw [in] constraints and surprises, and evaluate how the person reacts. If they're only well prepared beforehand versus if they are nimble on their feet and adapt, the interviewer can make a distinction.

Interviews are also less about the rudimentary stuff these days. It's more about how you adjust to new constraints thrown at you, because that's more applicable to the job and we're assessing these finer aspects of the role rather than the rudimentary. That's not to say that other stuff is not important. It's still super important.

Interviewing is imperfect. There are a lot of false negatives. There are false positives. It depends on what you want to favor as a company, whether it's more costly to hire the wrong person or miss out on a potentially good hire. Companies are probably thinking about that more and more because there's definitely a weird situation with supply and demand that also affects how interviewing is happening. There are a lot of PM roles, but at the same time, it's hard to find the right people. The more complex the job gets, it becomes more difficult to assess whether someone will be good at the job.

In your experience, how does product management differ across different types of digital products?

Khalid: From what I've seen, there are a few things that determine your day to day, what that will look like. One is the company, and of course, the title can be different. At Microsoft, for example, it's the "Program Manager" that does the product management job. If we consider the part of the job that is what to build and why, roadmapping, brainstorming, and then the project management aspect of it, the way I see those differ is a function of a few things. One is, where in its lifecycle is the product that you're working on? Is it closer to 0–1 or is it more 10–1,000? That will greatly determine your experience because, in the earlier stage, there's more ambiguity, less-defined metrics, and probably less history. That's different work and mentality than 100–1,000 when your product has product/market fit but the nature of the work is more about optimization.

Size of team will also change what your job looks like. If you have fifteen engineers, you don't have the time or energy to dig into every single project. Your work is more about coordination and cross-functional alignment, versus if you have three or four engineers and a smaller team, you're probably going to be more involved with the details of each project.

I've seen those two variables really impact what your day to day looks like and those would differ at the different companies based on the company or the position in the company. I would also say that there are companies where, as a PM, you have the most authority in terms of decision making compared to other functions like engineers or designers. There are companies at which the opposite is true, where design would have the most authority, and there are companies that are in the middle. One hint to gauge what to expect is to look at the background of the founder or CEO, are they a designer by trade, engineer, or Product person, their background or approach will tend to permeate the company.

Facebook is maybe somewhere in the middle. I would say that [at] Amazon or Zynga, the PM is driving more of the decision making. At Snapchat, I would say that maybe Design is more empowered. There's a few ways to figure that out. You can look at the CEO because that person's background or approach tends to permeate in the company. At Facebook, Mark is a Product guy but he's also an engineer, so such is the company. At Google, the CEOs were originally engineers and it's an engineering-first company. At companies like Amazon and Uber, they probably would put more value on the PM decision because there's a business aspect to decisions and less so a tech aspect. Companies that are more about technical innovation will probably weigh more on engineers. Look at the CEO and look at what the company is trying to do.

Over the course of your Product career, how have you seen product management evolve?

Khalid: I think one thing that has changed in the discipline over time, is maybe in the past there was more emphasis on the visionary thing. As a PM, you had to have all the answers. Over time, the problems have become more complex and more ambiguous such that no one person probably has the answer. Then your edge as a PM is, really, how can you make the best of everyone around you to be able to find a solution, versus being the Steve-Jobs-type CEO. I think there will always be a need for that kind of person. I think there will always be people like that who'd do great things, but on average, people overestimate how much you have to be like that versus not.

The role is evolving in such a way that it moves less so from the Steve Jobs model to more of a collaborative approach.

Matt Salazar

Head of Growth and Product Management, Epic Games (Previously Nike Digital)

What does product management mean to you?

Matt: That is really philosophical. It's a profession, not a position. People have almost diluted it down to this particular thing in an agile operating model where you have a product manager doing a purview of functions, but it's much bigger than that.

It's a profession that really values solving consumer problems through data insight and leading a team, often without influence. PMs are problem solvers in the same way engineers are. They just take a different angle to it. It's a new profession . . . if you think about the wave that's only happened maybe in the last twenty or thirty years at best, before that it was very just IT-heavy infrastructure, right? Technology development was more waterfall, a lot more prior requirements. There was less need to have someone obsess on a daily basis [about] how consumers were reacting to your product.

After the internet boom, the first dot-com boom, you saw the modern product manager emerge and you saw the need for that role grow. We were still defining what a product manager is in maybe the last fifteen years. It derived from that ethereal need that each company had, and then all of a sudden you started standardizing across industry and saying, "Okay, that's an actual role and an actual profession that people should be going after."

You've had some interaction with the folks on the physical product side. Have you learned anything from them that you've applied to digital product management?

Matt: It's surprisingly similar. There's a story in *Shoe Dog* about one of the first Nike employees, Jeff Johnson. They'd go out to the track and they'd just give away free shoes, let athletes run around the track in them, and then get feedback that they'd write on index cards. That's literally product management. If you think about the analogy, that's the same thing any digital product manager does nowadays but, instead of doing it one user at a time, he or she is doing it at scale with a million people. Now we can segment and, instead of giving everyone the red shoes, some get the blue shoe, and then we evaluate the difference in user response.

Earlier in my career, we probably over-indexed on data. Most of the mature PMs I knew started realizing that. We were missing some of the context and emotional resonance of why. That's what you really get through user testing, user interviews, reading reviews, reading the forums, and so on. If you think about our product life cycles at Zynga, every week or two we were releasing one or more new features. We were on this cadence because the retention curves were so brutal on the backside that if we weren't keeping people on this content flywheel, we were screwed. Consequently, we over-indexed on immediate signals rather than the long-term signals.

With most products out there, engagement frequency is lower. You're not going to have someone do eight sessions a day on a financial-services product, but the user lifetime is a lot longer. The longer the horizon and the longer the consumer journey, the more deliberate you can afford to be about the futures you need and you have a lot more time to synthesize the qualitative and quantitative. Data was really useful for, and is still the best for, optimization. We put a feature out there, it'll help us to optimize. What we all know that the data was terrible for is generating the new idea you're going to bring to the market, or understanding the why—the consumer need. That has to be the first hypothesis.

Sometimes the data will give you that, but sometimes you have to talk to people; because the data will constrict your frame of analysis versus taking a step back and seeing a broader view of the true consumer insight.

What other wisdom and insights have you gleaned over the years, as you've spent more time in Product and the profession has evolved?

Matt: Product is both art and science. You have to have a blend. I've seen Product come from the other side of pure art and it's like you're not using any data. When you start developing a product without a measurable objective or KPI to help back up your insights, you run the risk of just embracing [the] opinions of the most senior person in the room. Or you're doing user-insights testing and extrapolating conclusions from a focus group of four people that is not a representative sample of your entire user base. Extracting too much insight in a situation like that can be dangerous. It's when all these tools are taken to an extreme that you can make some really bad decisions.

What do you like best about product management?

Matt: Well, also going back to your earlier question, one of the things I really enjoy about the profession is that it's becoming ubiquitous. Just look at what you're doing now, even just within our peer group, the different industries we're in, but all still working in product management, right? You can do something in food delivery, you have Facebook, and the traditional Silicon Valley tech companies. You have now companies that were not natively digital, like Nike, coming into product management. It's becoming a career that you have a lot of breadth in and application into different problem sets.

I've found that even when I change companies and roles, I can still transfer seventy to eighty percent of what I do, even if it's a different industry, because the core is the same and what it teaches you about consumer empathy—thinking about holistic analysis, your role as a leader through influence and communication, and your drive to be just naturally curious—do not change that much. That has kept it exciting for me. I have a little bit of ADD, so I like interesting problems. I can't imagine being a lawyer, doing the same thing over and over and over again.

There's some specialization, especially within the junior ranks, but I think that's still congruent with career mobility; because even if you don't have an entrepreneurial background, you can still be doing a bunch of different things at different places. I still think that there is a core PM skill set that becomes applicable in almost any situation. If you say you're looking for an entrepreneurial PM, they could be an entrepreneurial PM doing healthcare. I feel like the skill sets are much more transferable across industries because it's more of an approach and a way of thinking, versus deep industry knowledge.

Product managers are expected to be naturally curious, so you could pick up that industry, that particular sector or industry knowledge, pretty quickly.

Does that mean that you are more or less recruiting the same types of people that you did much earlier in your career?

Matt: I focus on the same values and general skill-set type but I do value the variety of expertise. If I think about our Central Product Management [CPM] team at Nike, the commonality of threads there is that everyone has a solid PM background. They know how to do data analysis. They know how to do synthesis of qualitative and quantitative data. They know how to have consumer empathy, which translates into being able to prioritize and understand where the consumer needs are. They're able to communicate and influence. Those traits are table stakes.

All that said, the angles they come from can be very different. Having a well-rounded product team makes for the strongest product team. Initially, I wanted people with more of a technical background, who perhaps built data infrastructures from the ground up in a startup environment. I've had people with more experience on the front-end-consumer side, taking a product to market and rapidly iterating. That's also useful. Then you have people who have more commerce and marketing capabilities. We were trying to build (for CPM), commonality of thought, intent, and approach—and a sense of what good looks like—but we wanted different backgrounds and varied experiences because we needed a wealth of different angles from which to attack problems. CPM needs to be kind of a Swiss Army knife, a commando team that can succeed in any situation. We had a bench where I could plug in the right person for the right situation despite a very small team.

How do you and PMs on your team continue learning beyond what you see and research on the job? Are there go-to resources? Books, blogs, experts?

Matt: I think Product is one of the hardest things to pick up on. We don't have a Stack Overflow for PM specs, right?

To advance on the PM side, PMs need to do some heavy synthesis. Reading a lot of blogs, reading the news. Looking at industry data, like App Annie. I'm always on there looking at trends. *Along with the news, where are there correlations and connections?*

I think some of the best things, if I can find them, are product deconstructs. I'm trying to get smarter about China, Chinese-user patterns, and what's working there. I found a few good sites that do a lot of deconstructs. Any PM is going to have to understand China. China is truly not like the rest of the world. The Chinese consumer is distinct. Because of China's market size and market power, PMs will need to be really sharp in understanding what you need to do to be successful there.

When you have a new PM start on your team, is there a set of resources that you give them? How do you help them become the type of PM that you want them to be?

Matt: For a brand-new PM, I don't expect them to have PM experience or, at most, maybe they worked for two months as a PM for an internship. I start putting them in situations where they could start getting product reps. One of the advantages we had at Zynga was rapid iteration and many releases over short periods of time. It's a lot harder at non-gaming companies because the product life cycles are longer and the features [are] more involved and more complex.

How do you create situations such that they can get reps on and become a PM quickly? You want them working on some features because they're never going to learn if they aren't in the weeds and partnering with engineers. You also assign analysis of features that have just launched, doing growth-modeling work to understand what the key levers are and what will really drive your KPIs.

And you can start giving them feedback, "Okay, well, what about this? You just told me their onboarding flow is great. Why is it great? It has twelve steps. Tell me why you think it's great, and can you justify it?"

What I also like is having some experienced PMs do deconstructs, because they bring relevant experiences to us, and have a fresh pair of eyes on what we may be blind to in our own products or apps. At some point you're in the weeds so much, you may have thought about a problem, but you put it on the back burner. A new PM can come in and start tearing apart your product and saying, "Why did we do this? Why did we do this?" You either justify it and say, "Well, we do this because here's some context that you probably don't have. Or, you're absolutely right. Sh**. We should do something about that."

What are some other fundamentals that a new PM needs to learn ASAP?

Matt: I want some of the core elements of how you build good products. Some of the elements around hooks and habit formation. You've got to understand habit formation groups. You've got to develop consumer empathy because you can't design products just for yourself. How do you get someone in the right mindset to be able to approach that problem? I think that's always a common thing.

Growth modeling—active users, how a funnel works, and why active users—is one of the most valuable metrics you have versus downloads and installs. That's a big shift from anyone coming from a Marketing context, because they think it's just about reach and they're done. Active users really force you to think about Product as a life cycle and as an enduring service. I think it's a big change.

There are other things that make a good PM that you can't teach. You've got to have natural curiosity. You can't teach natural curiosity. The concept of the "product manager as CEO" is bullsh**. Product manager as a quarterback and as someone who has to rally the team together toward a common goal, and helping synthesize for the team, and leading a product, inspiring a production vision—all of those are absolutely a PM's job, but it's all going to be through influence.

I think as our experiences are becoming more intertwined and more complex with the physical world, or operational, product management requires more lead time and collaboration to make sure you can actually make the consumer journey successful. We've actively deprioritized features because other areas of the org weren't ready. It's okay, we go do something else. Let's get the value out some other way.

I hope people view product management more as a calling or a passion, rather than thinking, "Well, it pays pretty good. Blah, blah, blah. I get to feel important. Blah, blah, blah." I do hope more people are seeing it as a calling because they are passionate about trying to change consumer behavior for the positive. Maybe that's a little naïve. To be truly good at Product for the long term, you've got to make it feel like a calling, you've got to have the passion for it.

Christina Grimsley

Product Manager, Airbnb

To kick things off, what does product management mean to you?

Christina: To me, it is being in love with technology. Product management is about figuring out the problems your customers have, and figuring out ways to help solve those through technology.

How do you do that, on a daily basis?

Christina: You spend a lot of time listening and talking to your customers, getting to know who they are, it boils down to understanding the wide spectrum of people using your product and figuring out what's important to them, what frustrates them, what they really love, and even the emotions they experience while using your product. Once you know your customer, then you spend time figuring out how you might add in different tools or features or build apps and websites to make their lives simpler and better.

It sounds like you're doing a lot of user research. Are you speaking directly to customers or are you speaking more with internal stakeholders?

Christina: Research is key to understanding your customers. The majority of my past product management experience has been in building tools and platforms for internal users, mainly tooling for support agents so they can better solve problems for external customers. Building for internal users is unique in that you have instant access to your customers at any time. Currently, I'm working more on user-facing products, but I still conduct tons of research talking to end users, both with Airbnb customers and folks who have never used Airbnb before. I learned how to build products based on speaking directly with customers. Let me share some examples:

When I was at Uber, we were building tools for in-person driver support centers all around the world. These were like the "genius bar" for Uber. I would often just sit and watch people come into these centers - we used to refer to this as "walking the floor." I would observe to see what problems drivers were having but also to understand what the experience was like in person. Why did someone come to get support in-person? It wasn't particularly easy, so why in person versus sending an email to get the same answer? When someone walked into a support center, what were they expecting? How long did they have to wait? How were they expecting to be able to check in or to see someone to talk to? What kind of things were they interested in? Was it vehicle financing to get a new car or did they have an issue they were trying to resolve with a payment? I spent a lot of time just talking to drivers. That type of research-led, customer-centric approach has continued to be a focus throughout different roles within product management.

When I started working with support agents, I had to fly to Manila and fly to India to conduct the same kind of research, but we always prioritized shadowing agents. Your customer should be top of mind when developing product and a support agent is a unique one. Your average product manager in Silicon Valley might think, "Hey let's use all these really fancy tools and machine learning features, that'll be really cool," but The technical aptitude of your user is a really important thing to understand. We ran into many challenges by building for Silicon Valley instead of building for, say, a support agent in Manila. So that's been a huge part of working on internal and customer-facing tools—a big focus on user research.

As you speak with internal stakeholders, customer support teams, et cetera, about the pain points that they're encountering and you start to see things emerge, how do you prioritize what to work on? When we think about product management for end consumers in a consumer context, we often have a lot of data supporting which areas, if we were to solve those pain points, might have the most impact. It can be a little bit harder, internally. Are you still trying to use a data-driven approach to determine what you work on first or is it more based on the instincts of the product and design teams or perhaps influence of the leaders that you're working with?

Christina: It depends on the stage of the product, because I've had both. When I first started, I was building out the products for the in-person driver support centers. Ourdata was decentralized and hard to string together because we were using third-party tools, kind of jerry-rigged together. We knew some basic things like the number of people coming in, the wait time, but we didn't have a lot of instrumentation across all the different tools that we were using. So, a lot of what we prioritized and what we built was based on instinct and experience of working in similar environments, like leveraging my experience in Apple retail. We took a lot of inspiration from the Genius Bar experience, for example how they moved from managing everything on Macs to being mobile first and mobile forward. That was a priority so support specialists could move around a store and think about what the experience would be like there.Early on, it was instinct,research and building quickly to see what we could stand up that worked, then iterating.

There were also foundational features that needed to be in place for anything to work.

After I moved into more mature product areas, like the platforms for all channels of support at Airbnb and Uber,and focused, where we had thousands of agents with millions of tickets every year, data became a much more important part of product development.

You were discussing some differences between consumer-facing PMs and PMs working on internal products. Do you think that lateral movement between consumer to internal PM and vice versa is easy? Or what would be a struggle for a PM to change roles like that?

Christina: It depends on the company and your scope, but I think a lot of the frameworks and principles are the same. Internal PMs have some of the benefits of having a very close relationship with customers, because they are your peers, the people you work with everyday.. Understanding user research or seeing a trend in data and not understanding what's going on, you can look to your left, look to your right, or set up a Zoom call to ask some of those questions, which you can do in a consumer-facing role, but you do more educated guessing and infer from data versus asking questions and getting more insights from those personal relationships.

Christina, we'd love to hear about your journey to becoming a PM. What inspired you and then how you made the transition.

Christina: I was always interested in product, but I would credit my transition to a happenstance tour that I gave to a group product manager. He had been at Facebook for a really long time, had just joined Uber, and was taking over the support products team. He wanted to see support in action, so he came to do a tour and to see what was going on at our Greenlight Hubs. Again, in order to see agents in action typically, you had to fly to Manila or fly to India, and it was a little bit more of an investment than driving down the street. I did a tour of the support centers with him, walking him through what I had done to help build out these third-party apps to support the in-person driver experience. As we were talking about what we had done and my vision for the future,, he turned to me and asked, "You sound like a PM. Have you ever thought about product management?"

I said, "I love technology. I think about these things all the time, but I'm not an engineer. I've never worked directly with engineers." He laughed and responded, "I'm not an engineer." He had come from a marketing background and talked a lot about the fact that there was not one type of background required to be a product manager. That one conversation was a spark. I ended up following up with him, having lunch and asking if he was serious about what he had said. We ended up talking for a while about the job and what it would take, in terms of preparation and process. That conversation was my foot in the door, having someone recognize my potential and then setting up some conversations internally about how to make the transition.

At that time, there wasn't a formal process at Uber for a person to transition into product management, but several folks had completed what were called PM "trials." Those trials were internal transfers who stepped into the product management role for a period of time, performed in the job, then interviewed for a formal transition into the product organization. My move into product was really from that serendipitous moment - I happened to give a tour to a new leader who was in need of a product manager to join his team. The company was starting to build out all of the tooling, including check-ins and appointments, in this area where I was the expert. I knew the data like the back of my hand and was already working with 600+ managers of these sites around the world. I knew my customer really well. I knew the processes that could benefit from technology because I had created the standard operating procedures. There was a clear need that I could fill, so it ended up being the perfect transition at the perfect time.

Did you interview with internal leaders ? What else did you have to do before and during the actual process?

Christina: It was not a very formal process when I started, but successful transitions like mineI helped to formalize the trial process. To start, I had to have a sponsor. Anyone doing a trial had a product director or higher sponsor throughout the process. I was then moved into the product organization reporting to a group product manager. I would transition into the new role and function as a PM, working with engineers, designers, research, data science, the whole deal. The expectation was this trial would last for about six months, then I would have an opportunity to interview and formally move roles. It was tricky because while ideally I could be focused only on this new product role during the trial, I also had my "old" job to do and retained my former title while still in the trial period. The idea of that trial was that I would be doing the PM job, not my old job, which didn't really happen.

At the end of the trial, you'd have a work product to share and could say, "here is what I did over a quarter or two quarters." That was the benefit of this trial period - you could speak to what work you had actually done and could have cross-functional teammates attest to your skills, as opposed to getting the role by being really great at interviewing. So, after six months, I did a full interview process with multiple GPMs and directors, who all had to sign off on the transition.

What did you do during the trial period to ensure that you would be successful and that you would pass this gauntlet at the end?

Christina: The trial was a real opportunity to focus on the work and get to know what it's like to work with engineers, how you leverage data scientists, that design is your right hand. Because I had such deep experience and expertise in the product that I was owning, I was able to focus on these "net new" aspects of the work, as opposed to thinking about what was going to happen at the end of the trial.

I will say that, when I got closer to the interview process, I did a lot of prep. I practiced interviewing with anyone who would give me the time of day and did a ton of research and reading online. That was the first time I read *Cracking the PM Interview*. I ran through case questions over and over and over again. I didn't have as much mentorship throughout the six month trial process that was focused on what the interview would be like. It was just doing the job.

What was most difficult about being a PM? Did anything surprise you?

Christina: There's definitely a learning curve to figuring out how to work with all the different functions. For example, I'd never done sprints before. I had never done agile or scrum or keeping track of very small tasks and figuring out how to measure other people's work as closely as you do as a PM. Within operations, you might try to set deadlines and say, "Oh, I think this is going to take eight hours, or this might take four weeks," but it's squishier. The level of precision within product management was very, very different.

I was super lucky because I was partnered with a phenomenal engineering manager who really took me under his wing and taught me about how to work with engineering, how to ask the right questions, how to manage sprints, explained both what he needed from me as his product partner and what he would provide as an engineering partner.

I think that mentorship from an engineering manager was integral to what made me successful. Having mentors within the functions that you work very closely with as a PM is ideal if you haven't had the experience before. They can help you learn the product development cycle, like understanding what a PM does versus what a designer does versus what an engineering manager does, and figuring out how you work together. That ebb and flow is a little bit different than in other roles that I've had. There are also the basics, like to be successful, you need to understand how to work well with people on a team and teams of varying sizes, depending on what you're working on and what you're trying to deliver.

What do you find are the most challenging aspects of working in a product? Or most frustrating?

Christina: Product can be tough because you're often not really in control. You are *seen* as the go-to person and the keeper of the keys, like you're the one person that is able to make something happen or decides when to *not* make something happen. But behind the curtain, you are at the mercy of many other people. There's a lot of work involved. I'm not saying that a PM doesn't do anything, but you're not in as much control as it may appear to people externally. It's hard. I think the PM role is romanticized as the "CEO of your product," but there's more to it that folks new to the role or tech sometimes take the hard way.

You are in charge of driving a team forward, trying to figure out how to get a group to work really well together, orchestrate timelines, and inspiring a team to *want* to build a feature or build a product.

What makes the difference between a more junior PM versus a more senior, or even very senior, PM?

Christina: The obvious answer is experience and time in role or working at a tech company, working within a particular industry. How much scope you're actually owning often increases as you become more senior,if you own a feature within an App versus owning an entire platform.

Do you think there's any mindset or fundamental things that you learn or that change as you become more senior?

Christina: Yes - early on in my career, I was more focused on execution. What was shipping, when it was shipping, and what the results looked like at launch. Now, I think I'm more focused on strategy and collaboration, setting cross-organizational goals, and getting many different teams working toward an end state. That means spending more time influencing and leading versus just focusing on what you ship within your team. As you shift to a more senior role, you also shift to thinking more about the big picture and how to tie things together across teams..

You've worked at two big tech companies. How has the way that you've practiced product changed from Uber to Airbnb? That could be personal, but maybe there are also cultural differences between the two places that are in play.

Christina: Uber was incredibly data-driven, almost to an extreme. When I say "almost" I mean that even if something seemed like the right thing to do, if the data didn't support it, it was unlikely that the team would move forward. Data really ruled the decisions, which was great in some ways because the decision maker was clear - it was the data and the experiment results. As a PM, that makes your job easier in many ways, as the goal posts are very clear. Whatever the numbers showed you, that's what ended up happening. Now, you had to spend time making sure you set the right targets or goals and that the metrics you measured were the right ones. But assuming you had laid the groundwork, if that data supported your product, you were good to launch.

I saw a side of that data-driven culture at Uber that I *didn't* love. As we grew, our support costs were growing at the same pace. With the type of hockey stick growth we experienced at Uber, it quickly became clear that this type of cost wasn't sustainable and that we needed to invest in cost cutting. That became the number one focus - cost. Instead of thinking about the customer experience, focusing on features or service that prioritized customer satisfaction, we shifted focus solely to automation, chatbots to reduce contacts, deferring from more high-touch to low cost support channels. These things are not necessarily bad, but balance is important. That steadfast focus on driving down cost meant the team's commitment to the customer experience took a backseat. As someone who had spent their career passionate about support and how it can be a differentiator to the customer, I struggled to prioritize cost over user experience.

That's why when looking for my next role, I sought out a company that had that balance - focused on both data and the customer experience.

It's interesting to have seen a more data- and engineering-driven culture at Uber versus what I would call a design- or creativity-led company at Airbnb. Airbnb is very design-driven, which may not be surprising since two of the co-founders are designers. That culture creates a huge focus on research and people. It prioritizes the user experience and emphasizes the "right" thing to do. But there can be a lot of variability in that, which means that it can be harder to make decisions and hard to make decisions fast. There's a lot more negotiation, persuading, and conversation that PMs need to engage in versus simply saying, "Here are our experiment results. This is what we will do, because it is the goal that we set, and this is what makes sense."

It's pretty widely known that Airbnb has a stronger design-led culture than some of the other big tech companies. However, across tech, there's been a little bit of a pull back from data-driven towards data informed. Would you say that's accurate from what you've seen and experienced as well?

Christina: Yeah. And just trying to have a more mindful approach to how data is used, like giving customers more control over their data and keeping privacy top of mind. I started at Uber before the "more balanced" data-informed era. So, it may look a little bit different today.

PART 5

PM Glossary

Product Sense uses a variety of industry and product-specific terms that constitute a common language amongst product managers and throughout the tech and business world. Familiarizing yourself with these terms will serve you well as you prepare for an interview, complete a take-home exercise, or step into your first job as a PM. Here, we have compiled and alphabetized these terms and concepts so that you can easily reference them.

Acceptance Criteria: Conditions of a feature or product that need to be met in order for a feature to be considered complete. Usually included in PRDs or other product management planning documentation within a distinct section. *See also:* PRDs/Specs.

Acquisition: The term used when talking about how customers find the product or feature. What channel did they come through (such as SEO, paid, or organic)? Acquisition is considered the top of the funnel, where users first interact with the product.

Activation: A user may become activated in a number of ways, and this is generally when they start to fully experience the feature or product. Activation may be considered to be in effect after the user signs up, makes a post, or creates a group.

Active User: A user who is currently using the product. The product team will define what an "active" user is, and the PM will report all available data pertaining to "active" users. The exact criteria for an active user may vary from product to product; for example, some teams might consider an active user to be someone who has used the product at least once during the last thirty days while others might use a more generous ninety-day period.

Agile Development: The process of developing software in which there is a continued cycle of discovery (i.e., quick and early releases), and iterative and incremental development. Agile development is the most frequently adopted engineering process in the modern tech landscape. *See also:* story points, waterfall development.

ASO: App store optimization, which means ensuring that your mobile app's page in an app store such as the iOS App Store or the Google Play Store has great content and is formatted in ways such that it will receive more preferential treatment from Apple/Google and will yield a higher rate of downloads by users visiting the page.

Benchmarks: A standard or point of reference against which products, KPIs, or user experiences may be compared or assessed.

Best Practice/Differentiator/Table Stakes: A best practice is a feature or process that is generally accepted industry wide as a good optimization or inclusion for a product. A differentiator is a feature that is unique to a product that the competing products do not have. A table stakes feature is a feature that is required for a product to meet the basic expectations of a customer.

Calibrated: This means that the company placed their interviewers into a training program, and coached them to conduct interviews according to a certain criteria (which includes the four categories listed above), all before ever sitting across from you in a PM interview.

Churn: Refers to users who stop using a product. The PM will report all available data pertaining to churn. *See also:* friction *and* funnel.

Cohorts/Personas: Cohorts are sets of users grouped by a measurable characteristic, such as the date or month they became active, or how they behave when using a product. A persona is a narrative-based characterization of a user that highlights certain problems and pain points they might have. Both of these terms are used when articulating for whom a team is building a new feature. *See also:* active user *and* churn.

Conversion: The step in the funnel which signals the user got the value that they wanted, and then converted in some way. Converting can mean a number of things, such as purchasing something, retaining for a long period of time, or inviting a friend. *See also:* active user, funnel.

Dependencies: Changes or features that must be completed in order for development on another change or feature (possibly being worked on by another team) to proceed.

Edge Cases: A section in the feature's PRD, usually outlining the details of how a specific feature would behave in less common scenarios. For example, "If the user has no valid credit card, show them this specific error message." *See also:* PRDs/Specs.

Engagement: How frequently and how much usage an average customer gets out of the product within a defined period of time.

FAANG: This acronym refers to Facebook, Amazon, Apple, Netflix, and Google—large, public, tech companies that hire many engineers and product managers using consistent and predictable processes and criteria. These companies also typically offer high total compensation to their new employees.

Freemium: Freemium represents the business model of certain tech products that are free to use initially, but monetize through a specific purchase type down the line, such as an upgrade. This term typically refers to games, e.g. *Candy Crush Saga*, which is free to play but in which players can elect to pay for additional lives or moves in order to complete a puzzle or extend their play time.

Friction: A user experiences friction when they are using a product and run into issues, or other nonintuitive experiences, that causes him to complete a task at a slower pace or halts his progress completely. *See also:* churn *and* user flow.

Funnel: A funnel refers to the sequence of steps a user must go through in order to complete a specific action. For example: When purchasing shoes on a website, a user would first search for and find an item, then select a style and size, and finally enter his payment information. Funnels are often analyzed to determine where users are dropping off, or leaving the funnel without completing their objectives or making a purchase. *See also:* activation, churn, friction, *and loops.*

KPIs (Key Performance Indicators): The metrics (usually data) that help measure the business or product health.

Lifetime Value (LTV): The average amount of revenue that customers spend over the course of their time with a business (owning or utilizing a product).

Loops: Loops are similar to a funnel, in that they are the steps that a user takes in order to complete a specific action. However, with loops the steps are repeatable and are done regularly. For example,

Farmville's loop is planting crops, watering them, and then harvesting them, which gives the player more resources to expand their farm. *See also:* funnel.

Minimum Viable Product (MVP): The smallest amount of features or scope required to launch a new product. Teams will often make the lowest initial investment in a product or an idea—in order to release it sooner and follow its progress as a test—before expanding and making a bigger investment.

North Star Metric: The primary metric that is the "guiding light" for knowing whether a team is making progress toward achieving its vision and, ideally, supports the company's bottom line or other strategic objectives. Just as the North Star in the sky helps people navigate when they are lost, this metric can provide feedback on whether a release makes a positive (or negative) impact.

Opportunity Cost: The loss of potential gain from a certain feature or features when an alternate feature is chosen for development. For example, if you have limited engineering resources to allocate toward building new features in a given quarter, then you may have to forgo completing some of your roadmap items. The opportunity cost will be the value those deprioritized features might have created.

Pain Point: An obstacle that a user encounters when using a product.

PRDs (Product Requirement Documents)/Specs (Specifications): These terms are used interchangeably to mean the written documentation a PM prepares to communicate the requirements a feature will need in order to achieve a specific outcome. *See also:* acceptance criteria, edge cases.

Prioritization Framework: A tool used by PMs to weigh features against another.

Product Audit: An exercise that PMs use to evaluate what a competing (or otherwise preexisting) product offers in terms of features, user flows, and areas of improvement. Very beneficial when determining what to build and also a good way for a PM to strengthen her product sense.

Quality Assurance (QA): The process of testing software before release to identify and fix (or prioritize for fixing) any bugs or errors. Also the title of the person who holds this role on the team.

Retention: The likelihood that users will come back to the product after a specific amount of time.

Roadmap: A prioritized collection of features and improvements that have been aligned on and are in progress, or planned for the future.

SEO: An abbreviation for Search Engine Optimization. This is the process of managing web pages so that Google (or other search engines) can rank the pages according to specific target keywords for which a user might search. Includes creating appropriate headers, optimizing metadata, and ensuring the site is up to Google's standards.

Stakeholder: A person with a vested interest in a project. Someone who invests in its success has a viewpoint on the direction it will take.

Also someone with whom a PM might need to align a product or feature's goals and plans before moving to the next phase. As a PM, you will likely have several (or even many) different stakeholders.

Story Points: A term used in agile development that refers to the "engineering cost" of building a feature (typically in the form of the number of days it will take one engineer to complete the task). *See also:* agile development.

T-shirt Costing: The assigning of values such as "S," "M," "L," etc., by a PM or a team, as a means to indicate the expected effort that will be required from a product development team to complete a change or feature.

Technical Debt: This term refers to the "debt" incurred when an engineering team makes the decision to use an imperfect functional design in order to expedite a feature's delivery. Accumulated technical debt makes creating future features or tweaks more difficult, but in the short term this may outweigh delaying a release. Eventually, teams will need to "pay" the debt (i.e., go back and fix the imperfect technical design), in order to create a more scalable architecture.

Trade-Offs: When two metrics or concepts are competing against each other, a PM will evaluate any advantages or disadvantages of electing each approach in order to prioritize which one the team will choose.

User Flow: A series of actions and experiences that a user encounters while using a product, often used in the context of describing an attempt to accomplish a particular goal or return a particular result.

User Story: A requirement for a feature written from the perspective of a prospective user. "As a user, I want to be able to sort the list of shoes from the lowest to the highest price." Doing this helps communicate to an engineering team what they should build, so user stories are often included in product requirement documents.

Validation: When a PM has a hypothesis about their users, and their users' needs, she will want to confirm this by validating those needs with data or user research.

Waterfall Development: An engineering process method in which different phases of development are structured sequentially, each depending on the previous one. For example, the design team completes their work first, then they hand it off to the engineering team, and when engineering is done they hand it off to the QA team. An alternative is agile development, in which the work is done collaboratively and in real time. Most modern product development teams operate using an agile approach but waterfall development may make sense in some circumstances. *See also:* agile development.

Wireframe: Rough sketches of what the flow of a feature might look like that help convey the idea to stakeholders or the rest of the product development team (also known as *mockups).*

Workflow: A user's daily actions to complete their work. Most often found in B2B settings, where the end user is an employee at another organization, who has daily tasks they need to complete (inside or outside of your product).

Zero to One: When something is built that previously did not exist.

Credits & Acknowledgements

Editor and Proofreader: Shawn Richardson

Designer: George Stevens

Advisors & Contributors: Adam Braus, Marshall Thomas, Mari Knudson

Interviewees: Christina Grimsley, Jon Mensing, Julia Panopoulos, Julie Zhou, Kevin Sung, Khalid Ashour, Matt Salazar, Nick Turley

Early Readers: Uche Ekeopara, Loan, Kelly Lydek, John Fontenot, Judy Bragg, Marcelo Garza, Sam Rim, Adrian Crook, Lisa & Scott Knudson, Biswajit Jena, Jake Lynch, Patrick Joliecoeur, Maggie Chen, Kristina Lee, Sue Rim, Stephen Fiehler, Chelsea Yaw, Wes Mann

Special Thanks & Shout Outs

From Peter

I first want to thank all those who continued to support me through a tumultuous 2020, one that had a large amount of personal and professional hurdles that I needed to navigate in addition to making progress on *Product Sense*. My immediate family (Scott, Lisa, Amelia, Sonja, and Mari) and my friends (especially Patrick, Evan, Joona, and Daniel) supplied tremendous support during a very challenging time.

I also want to acknowledge that I would know nothing about product management had it not been for my mentors and managers throughout my career: Janet Fong, Joe Traverso, Felix The, Stephen Sullivan, Adrian Crook, and Daniel Fine. Lastly, our editor Shawn: without her, our manuscript might not have been very readable at all.

I also want to give major props to my co-author, who never gave up despite pregnancies, job changes, and our constant bickering on minor stylistic preferences and general pedantry.

From Braxton

Is there ever a perfect time to write a book? When I started this project with Peter, I was living in Long Island City, I held a very stable job, and Sue had *just* learned that she was pregnant. Since that time, I moved to Brooklyn, left my stable job, and started a new and much-less-stable job, lost my new and much-less-stable job, advised three startups, had a daughter, started a new job, reactivated my CPA license, and prepared to move again. The vast majority of this took place during the COVID-19 pandemic and over just 1.5 years! If there *is* a perfect time in one's life to write a book, this was probably not it . . .

Peter Knudson, you are an amazing co-author. Would not have taken on this challenge without you. I'm so glad we had that conversation about our coaching experiences, realized that we both aspired to write a book about product management, AND THEN ACTUALLY WENT AND DID IT. I am in awe of the content you've written and everything I've learned (and reconsidered) about product management since we started this. I don't care if we sell a single copy of this book—it's been a great experience and I think we're both better writers and Product thinkers than we were when we started. I'm not at all oblivious to the fact that the lion's share of the more complex content in this book came straight out of your mind. Hopefully I was a good enough thought partner and foil that we made a better product together! I appreciate you, man.

Marshall Thomas, you have been, and always shall be, my friend. Really appreciate your very thorough read and detailed feedback on almost everything that we wrote. This book has many <u>lesser</u> mistakes than it otherwise would have. Looking forward to helping you edit *your* book someday!

Judy Bragg, I wouldn't be here without you, in more ways than I can count. Thank you for everything, all the time, forever. Dan Bragg, you're also pretty great—I know that you will immediately appreciate what I've done in this paragraph! ;-)

A very special thanks goes to Sue Rim. Without your patience over the last year, this book DEFINITELY WOULD NOT HAVE BEEN POSSIBLE. Not only did you share blunt feedback that helped us rethink a few sections, you've also been gracious enough to assume even *more* responsibility for raising our daughter while I've been goofing off writing a super-fun book about my career.

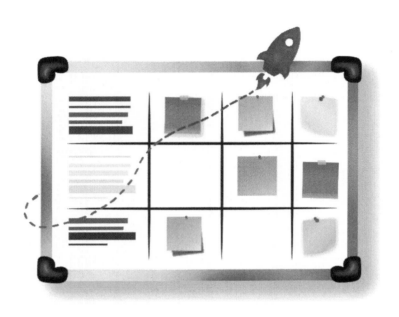

More resources and tips at

ProductSenseBook.com/Resources

Made in the USA
Coppell, TX
22 January 2025

44793439R00201